The Grouchy Grammarian™

*A How-Not-To
Guide to the
47 Most Common
Mistakes in English
Made by Journalists,
Broadcasters, and
Others Who Should
Know Better*

THOMAS PARRISH

BCA

This edition published 2003
by BCA
by arrangement with John Wiley & Sons, Inc.

CN 111983

Published by John Wiley & Sons, Inc., Hoboken, New Jersey
Published simultaneously in Canada

Design and production by Navta Associates, Inc.

For general information about our other products and services, please contact our
Customer Care Department within the United States at (800) 762-2974, outside
the United States at (317) 572-3993 or fax (317) 572-4002.

Wiley also publishes its books in a variety of electronic formats. Some content that
appears in print may not be available in electronic books.

Printed in Great Briain by Mackays of Chatham Ltd, Chatham, Kent

I'm not working in architecture, I'm working in architecture as a language, and I think you have to have a grammar in order to have a language. You can use it, you know, for normal purposes, and you speak in prose. And if you are good at that, you speak in wonderful prose. And if you are really good, you can be a poet.

—LUDWIG MIES VAN DER ROHE, 1955

The English language is exquisite and a source of delight.

—JOYCE CAROL OATES, 2001

Contents

The Grouch and I

{ i }

It wasn't any one thing that finally turned my old friend, the grouchy grammarian, into a strident activist. For a long time he had been minding his own business, he told me, with no desire to get into any arguments with anybody. I didn't completely believe him, to tell you the truth. For all his talk about loving a quiet life and trying to stay out of trouble, I knew he enjoyed a good fight.

What happened, exactly?

I had stopped by to see him one morning in March. Though he gave me as friendly a greeting as his nature permitted, his voice was heavy with depression. I saw nothing unusual in that, of course. Every time he picked up a newspaper or clicked on the TV, he would see or hear some blunder that would start him cursing reporters, editors, broadcasters, media executives, and, more fundamentally, the schools and colleges that had produced such bunglers. But today he seemed even more downcast—and therefore grumpier—than usual.

I asked him what the trouble was.

In just a few weeks it would be April, the old grump snapped, and he already dreaded its coming. Didn't I realize that TV newscasters, National Public Radio reporters, newspaper headline writers, and other media types would soon be telling us all, with infuriating repetitiveness, to set our clocks ahead on a certain Saturday night because "daylight *savings* time" was arriving? (When he chose to, he could speak in loud italics.) "*SavingS* time," he repeated, hissing the *S*. "There's no such damned thing, of course," he said; "the expression makes no sense at all. The correct term, *daylight-saving time*, describes a method of conserving, or *saving*, daylight by changing the clock rather than changing people's habits."

I knew that, and he knew I knew it, but we seemed to agree that he shouldn't risk a stroke through trying to repress his feelings.

"The rise of *savings* here," growled my gruff old friend, "is probably the result of this word's increasing use as a singular rather than a plural noun. Look at advertisers—they're the chief perpetrators." Riffling (not *rifling*) through his mail one day, it seemed, he had felt particular irritation when he came across a brochure with this message: "For only $19.95 (a $10 *savings*), you can receive a full-grain leather Shirt Pocket Briefcase." "It's only *one* saving!" he snarled. "*Savings* represents a plural idea, standing for the results of many individual acts of saving. We have a *savings* account, but buying something we need at a reduced price represents a *saving*."

As you can see, my friend not only had a snappish temperament, he had a strongly developed fondness for leaping into a lecture from a standing start.

Other incidents followed the savings affair as winter moved into spring. One evening, while the grouch and I were watching a basketball tournament game, he recoiled in horror when an otherwise competent basketball color commentator declared after a player intercepted a pass and started downfloor that there was "nobody between *he* and the basket."

Not long afterward, he heard another color commentator,

this one on baseball, offer the opinion that if a runner tagged out at second base had slid, "he *may* have been safe."

Spelling, too, concerned my friend. He plucked a clipping from a stack of papers and waved it at me. When it stopped fluttering, I saw from the type that it had come from the *New York Times*; the headline read "Profit Rises 10% at *Phillip* Morris." My friend also noted that another newspaper believes that the Duke of Edinburgh's first name is *Phillip* and that we once had a march king named John *Phillip* Sousa (the latter a belief shared at least once by the *Times Magazine*). "And the people at the Museum of Modern Art," he said with a kind of negative chortle, "think they know a composer named *P-h-i-l-l-i-p* Glass. They spelled it that way in one of the ads for that concert series they have in the summer."

When the grouchy grammarian heard an actor in a TV drama describe a souvenir as "a nice *momento*," he reacted with deep disgust. "Those people must think that the word is a fancy Spanish or perhaps Italian adaptation of *moment*," he barked. "But what in God's name would the idea of moment have to do with the idea of remembering? Actually, *memento* merely comes from the Latin verb *meminisse*—to remember."

I nodded, dutifully.

$$\left\{ \textbf{ ii } \right\}$$

"All these blunders!" the grouch said to me one day. "They're getting to me, Parrish, really getting to me! Just killing me! Where do they come from? Where in the hell do they come from?"

"Well," I said, "they may—"

"A general lack of information—that's it, damn it! And what an overall effect—anything but professionalism! Anything *but* professionalism! What did these people study in high school and college? Headline writing? Advertising techniques? No English, no history? Have they never loved words and ideas, the way a carpenter loves wood or a chef loves herbs? Didn't they want to know subjects and verbs, adverbs and prepositions, as the carpenter knows nails and sandpaper and hot glue? Have they never taken a sentence apart to see what made it run?"

I was about to respond to all these sizzling exclamation points and question marks with a little joke about verbs and herbs, but before I could get my tongue moving he gave me what amounted to a glare. "These are important questions, Parrish—damned important!" He paused. "You wouldn't disagree with me, would you?"

"No, sir, I certainly wouldn't. But—"

"But what?" His voice had a real crackle in it.

The time for jokes had clearly passed. I decided to take a bold step. I'd been thinking about it ever since the daylight-saving incident, and now seemed as good a chance as I would ever get.

"Well, sir," I said, "what are you going to do about it?" I meant was he just going to stump around and rumble and swear as he read his newspaper, just content himself with hurling invective at the faces on the TV screen? Settle for being nothing more than a complaining old sourpuss?

I didn't put it that way, of course, but I must have spoken clearly enough for the point to come through.

My friend hawed and harrumphed for a minute or two, while I sat quietly. It wasn't up to him to save the language, he declared, much as he loved it. Language had always had its Don Quixotes and always would have them, and all honor to them— but he didn't have to join their company. And it certainly wasn't up to him to try to educate the media. In any case, those people wouldn't pay any attention to him; they already knew everything, didn't they?

Beneath the surface, however, the recent run of blunders must have been working on him, pushing him to the brink. Yet I admit I felt a surge of surprise when, with a sort of terminal, the-die-is-cast *humph!* he said that well, perhaps . . . perhaps he could try being at least a little bit positive instead of wholly negative. (He meant, of course, a *very* little bit positive. He was, after all, a confirmed grump and a lifelong grouch. Actually, I felt, he was announcing his readiness for battle.) He would do no writing himself, of course; he had neither the inclination nor the time for that. But if I was foolish enough to think I could make a real contribution to the well-being of his beloved language, I was welcome to go through the clippings in his file folders—and swollen folders they were—and jot down some of the comments he had made about them, and others he might offer in conversation; I could pass this information along to the public in any form that seemed suitable to me.

Any work we produced would be prescriptive, of course; otherwise, said my friend, it would have no point. We would actually say that some usages are better than others and even that some are right and others are wrong. He readily conceded that prescribing in matters of grammar and usage has long been out of style in the world of linguistics, but "if you merely want description, just walk down the street, take a ride on the subway, go to the opera—you'll hear all kinds of people saying all kinds of things. That's not worth my time or yours, Parrish. You'll want to show your readers how the language is used by informed and thoughtful people, and why this is the best way. You'll be concerned with nothing less than craftsmanship, and you'll pay attention to accuracy and grace as well." He said this with a kind of professional pride. "You'll be producing a manual of practical correctness, and you'll have to do it negatively, of course, by showing mistakes—usages writers should avoid."

"A how-not-to manual," I suggested.

One more *humph!* "But philosophically, of course, just the opposite. That's what will give it any value it may have."

In all this talk, did the grouchy grammarian display a measure of conceit? Yes, he did. But, to his credit, he also revealed a surprising measure of compassion. "You don't want to shoot at the easy targets—the people at the local dailies and the small TV and radio stations. They have plenty of problems, of course, and they can certainly use your help. But almost all of the examples you'll see in these folders come from much higher up on the mountain: National Public Radio, the *New York Times*, the Associated Press, the History Channel, the broadcast TV networks, the big newspaper chains. These people are, or are trying to be, true professionals. They're supposed to serve as models for the rest of us. They're the ones who should welcome a simple manual, especially when they realize that they themselves have written a good part of it." He allowed himself a chuckle. "Not the best part, of course."

Later that evening, back home and sitting at my desk, I realized what a foolish chance I had taken. Suppose my friend had responded to my challenge by harrumphing around for a few minutes and then deciding to write his own book! What a catastrophe that would have been—not because of his ideas but because he could never have changed his personality in order to ingratiate himself with the public; he's incapable of even minor tinkering, and thus his personal style would have emerged as his writing style. Instead of spreading honey to catch flies, he would have expected the little creatures to appear in hordes, thirsty for vinegar. If they didn't, that would simply be their own loss.

So, given all that grouchiness, why did I put up with my friend? Why did I choose to spend time with him? I could learn a great deal from him, and that was important. But, beyond that, I think, one old book sums it up. Worn and shabby, with a slip of paper protruding from its pages, it caught my eye one day as we were sitting in my friend's little study, and when I picked it up I saw that it was a World War II–era book-club collection of Robert Browning's poems. I turned to the flagged page: "A Grammarian's Funeral"—I might have expected it! In a little introductory paragraph to this poem, the editor told readers that here "the humble scholar becomes a hero, a man of courage and steadfast purpose, successful in his failures." My friend had long ago added his own mark, by underscoring two of Browning's lines: "So, with the throttling hands of death at strife / Ground he at grammar." My friend sees himself in a dramatic light, no doubt, but, like the Renaissance grammarian in Browning's poem, he has remained steadfast, true to his star. To my friend, that old grammarian was certainly no dusty, hairsplitting scholar busying himself with insignificant minutiae of language. And even though in our talk about our project the grouchy grammarian showed little awareness of the tender sensitivities that characterize our touchy contemporary culture, he didn't encourage me to go after small and easily wounded game. He wanted to take on the big boys. That appealed to me, too. Why shouldn't I have some fun?

{ iii }

As soon as I began working on the project, I realized that my friend had his own special view of the sentence—a simple analogy that provided the basis for all his thinking. He saw it as a car engine, with its equivalents of pistons, valves, carburetor, distributor (as you would expect, this vision had come to him long before the development of fuel injection and computerized firing control), each specialized part working with all the others to move the reader or the listener from A to B, or, if necessary, from A all the way to Z. It was a rational entity, whose workings could be understood by anybody—you simply had to take the trouble to look. He had no particular stylistic bill of goods to sell—he seemed to like all levels of diction, from the mandarin

8 THE GROUCHY GRAMMARIAN

to the slangy. But if you didn't understand the working of the sentence, he said, you had no chance of achieving precision and clarity, and if you aimed for the elegant and the poetic but couldn't make subject and verb agree, you could produce nothing but mush. He preached internal harmony for all kinds of sentences, no matter what their content.

"Keep the book short," my friend said, "and don't start it with any kind of introduction. The mistakes and infelicities—and the corrections—are what's important. Just get right into the thick of things. In medias res, you know."

No introduction? I felt myself smiling. Very well.

Some time later, when I went to give him a sort of interim report, he wanted to know how many topics, as he called them, I had found. It was working out to more than forty, I told him.

"That many?" he said, in almost a wondering tone. "I didn't realize you were going to take them all."

I hadn't, I told him. I had taken those that popped up most frequently, as we had planned. The files held many more that I hadn't touched. Besides, a number of the topics were short and quite word specific. That seemed to satisfy him. When I told him that, as far as possible, I had arranged the items in the order in which the blunders seemed to annoy him, because I considered this about as good a measure of their relative importance as I was likely to find, I received the only words of praise—well, half-praise—I heard from him at any time during my work on the project. Almost smiling, he said, "I couldn't have done it much better myself."*

---

*Fortunately, my friend didn't insist that I produce a classic round number of topics; he had little concern about that kind of tidiness one way or the other. When I commented that a few of his points relating to efficiency and grace did not involve literal correctness, he agreed that instead of calling those particular usages errors, I might think of them as "infelicities to be cured."

THE
TOPICS

Think!

The grouchy grammarian instructed me to tell you at the beginning that he can't teach anybody every individual thing and neither can I, but that we can "damn well" try to hound you into THINKING. Hence I begin with his fundamental rule:

> *Think about what you're saying—*
> *know what it means and where it came from.*

Though this rule is general rather than specific, discussion of it gives us the chance to take a sort of overview of our subject. Besides, the principle suffers from such frequent violation, as the grouch likes to say, that it unquestionably belongs among the forty-seven topics: "You can't stress it too much, Parrish!" But too busy to heed it, you say? No time? Well, surely you're not too busy to wish to avoid appearing ignorant in public, are you? And maybe tomorrow, or one day soon, you'll have a boss or a teacher who doesn't believe that mediocre is good enough and will therefore expect more from you. In any case, spend some time with the following examples.

• • •

During a TV travelogue showing the wonders of a Utah ski resort, the commentator informed us that forty years ago "the population had dwindled to 1,000 people." Discussing an incident of urban unrest, an AP reporter noted that "blacks account for 43 percent of Cincinnati's population of 331,000 people." But what else could a *population* dwindle to or consist of besides "people," since that's what the word means? In each sentence, simply omitting "people" would have taken proper care of things.

The late evening news once declared that a certain luckless convict had been "electrocuted to death." Now that's true overkill, since *electrocute* means to execute by means of electricity. As the old grouch likes to say, pay attention to what words mean, and if you don't really know, look them up. Don't just take a stab at it. And, as noted above, don't plead lack of time as an excuse.

Don't forget *daylight savings time*, of course. A columnist commented in the *Sarasota Herald Tribune*: "Some may question how Daylight Savings Time contributes to the disintegration of our American Way of Life." Regrettably, however, the writer isn't bothered at all by the expression "Daylight SavingS Time"; he seems to be using it without thinking about it. He's simply objecting to what he professes to see as the undesirable social effects of "fast time," as people used to call DST.

And what about *rate of speed*? "The car smashed into the fruit stand while traveling at a high rate of speed." Anybody who has had junior high science or math should remember that speed *is* a rate, and in such sentences one rate is enough. Merely say "while traveling at high speed." Think! commands the grouch. He also suggests, in his own special style, that you remember what you once knew but have allowed to slip away.

A TV reporter informed us one evening that in 1938 "the country was in the grips of the Great Depression." She didn't mean, of course, that Americans of that era found themselves confined inside some set of giant economic suitcases—*grips*—but was simply referring to the Depression's strong grasp, or grip. As is often the case, she seemed to be employing a word without really thinking about its meaning—it was just a word. Sober narrators of historical programs dealing with that same era often tell us that something took place "at the height of the Depression." Such a sentence, of course, completely demolishes "Depression" as a figure of speech; what the narrators mean is the *depth* of the Depression.

A Knight Ridder columnist, writing in the early days of the Clinton administration, observed that the president's "softer" management style was "viewed with suspicion by those who don't *ascribe* to it." But *ascribe* is a word we use to make an observation about somebody else, and so it must have an object; you could, for example, *ascribe* softness to Clinton, but he himself must *subscribe* to a management style, an idea, or anything else.

Several years later, when management style had become the least of the Clinton administration's worries, Rev. John Neuhaus of the magazine *First Things* delivered himself of a uniquely ghastly comment on the president's personal problems: "It would be an enormous *emetic*—culturally, politically, morally—for us to have an impeachment. It would *purge* us" (*Washington Post*). As my grouchy friend responded, rather in the style of Samuel Johnson, "Americans may well offer profound thanks that we were not simultaneously hit by an emetic and a purge—both ends, so to speak, against the middle. The poor body politic might not have survived such a double assault."

In making points in relation to time, writers often fall into redundancy or even simple silliness. In a profile of the British writer-politician Jeffrey Archer, the *New Yorker* observed that as a young MP, Archer "seemed to have a promising future *ahead of him*." NBC-TV in Los Angeles produced a neat counterpart by telling viewers that an advertiser who had used Martin Luther King's "I Have a Dream" speech in a commercial (and thereby had stirred up quite a flap) planned to do more such ads and the audience should therefore "look for more historic figures *from the past.*" That, of course, would be a likely place to find historic figures, just as the future, for everybody, does, reassuringly, lie ahead.

A third member of this group is a photo caption bearing the information that FDR was "rarely seen in a wheelchair during his lifetime." Nor, one cannot resist adding, has the situation changed much since his death. (A curious phrasing often occurs in relation to death. The writer will assert something like "*Before* her death she wrote her reflections on changes she had seen during her lifetime." Well, this person could hardly have written these reflections *after* she died. A writer usually means in such a context "in the last year before her death," "shortly before her death," or something similar.)

The word *favorable* carries the idea of success, of moving toward a desired result. That's why a radio listener was startled to hear a fuddled disc jockey interrupt his music to warn his audience that "conditions are *favorable*" for the development of a tornado—favorable, perhaps, from the point of view of the incipient tornado.

"Two people were killed when a U.S. helicopter prepared for search-and-rescue duty crashed *accidentally* in neighboring Pakistan." Commenting on this tragic incident, the grouch wondered who could have supposed that the chopper might have crashed *purposefully*.

The arrangement of words in a sentence requires thought, too. You may need them all, but if you don't have them in the right order they will turn on you. Note this example from the *Tampa Tribune:* "Shortly after 3:30 p.m. Friday, Tampa Fire Rescue officials said they responded to a call from a resident at the Cypress Run Apartments . . . who said she heard a child crying after falling from the second-story window." "I see this kind of thing every day," the grouch had written in a snarly little note clipped to the paragraph, "but I have to admire anybody who's falling from a window but still can think about something besides his immediate fate."

A Web entrepreneur who marketed men's shirts embroidered with the words WIFE BEATER, thus offending the operators of women's shelters and the members of women's rights groups, declared that he had hatched this great idea after watching the TV drama *Cops*, which he said often shows people "in *sleeveless T-shirts*" being arrested for domestic violence. While shaking his head in disgust at this particular blend of commercialism and folly, the grouchy grammarian snorted that if it's sleeveless it's not a T-shirt, because the name comes from the shape; it's just a plain undershirt or, in some parts of the English-speaking world, a singlet. He conceded, however, that this point probably had not been of much concern to the saddened and infuriated women.

In a discussion of out-of-office U.S. presidents who decided to take up residence in New York, the *Times* observed: "Former presidents and vice presidents thinking about putting down roots in the Big Apple might do well to read E. B. White's famous essay, 'Here Is New York.' It divides the city into *three quadrants*" (lifers, commuters, and those who come to Manhattan in search of something). Three quadrants? E. B. White, one of the most urbane and graceful of writers, the creator of the *New Yorker*'s original style and tone, had said *three quadrants*? A quadrant is a fourth, not a third. How could he have done such a thing? "Is that the *Times*'s error," I asked the grouchy grammarian, "or did E. B. White really say that?" "I can't tell you," he said. "I couldn't imagine that White could do such a thing, but, you know, I was afraid to look it up and find out." I couldn't blame him.*

---

*White was innocent, of course. "There are roughly three New Yorks" is what he wrote.

"Over the last five years, the Casino Queen . . . has brought 1,200 jobs to this *predominately* black city of 42,000 people [East St. Louis] just across the Mississippi River from St. Louis." Or, "Hyaline membrane disease is a dangerous condition, found *predominately* in premature babies." These sentences, one from the *New York Times*, the other from a syndicated medical column, are hardly likely to confuse a reader, but the grouch nevertheless clipped them. The craftsmanly writer, he would say, prefers *predominantly*, which pairs with the adjective *predominant*; *predominately* he considers a slovenly impostor, since it has no counterpart adjective but is merely *-ly* hooked to the verb. He sees it as a second-class word.

My friend also detests such scramblings as the substitution of the adverb *somewhat* for the noun *something*, as in: "I have long been acknowledged as *somewhat* of an expert on sleep" *(Fort Worth Star-Telegram)*. You may be *somewhat* sleepy, but you can hardly be *somewhat* OF an anything. The *Los Angeles Times* committed the same blunder in informing us that "polo shirts have become *somewhat* of an American uniform," and the newspaper supplement *American Profile* joined in by describing the development of the proposed World War II memorial as "*somewhat* of a bureaucratic quagmire at times." Even the imparting of colorful personal information cannot cure this error: "I'm *somewhat* of a student of U.S. Cabinet secretaries. I have a tattoo of Elliot Richardson on my buttocks" (Tony Kornheiser, a columnist). *Somewhat* sloppy, all those items!

Metaphors and other figures of speech often do not receive the respect they deserve. For instance, a headline in the *New York Times* says: WRITING ABOUT RACE, WALKING ON EGGSHELLS—that is, proceeding warily in a delicate situation. This is nonsense. The real expression is *walking on eggs*. The idea is to tread so softly that you avoid turning those fragile eggs into nothing more than useless eggshells. Regrettably, an office supervisor in Texas showed no likelihood of making such an effort. Responding to complaints about his excessive cursing, he fired back with both barrels: "I'm tired of walking on (expletive) eggshells, trying to make people happy around here." Unfortunately, perhaps, even the expletive cannot rescue the metaphor; to save it, the boss needed undamaged (expletive) eggs. Just be kind to metaphors, the grouch likes to say, and they will repay you richly.

A radio news report described a certain government project as an *overwhelming failure*. But overwhelm means to turn over, to overcome by superior power. You can overwhelm something if you're being successful, but never if you're failing.

Old strong ("irregular") verbs continually cause trouble. Speaking of President George W. Bush's actions in relation to an electric-power crisis in California, an AP writer observed that "Bush has *tread* carefully." That brings to mind the possibility of a chorus enthusiastically giving us "Onward, Christian Soldiers" with the line "Brothers, we are treading where the saints have *tread*." Doesn't sound quite right, does it?

Sometimes writers don't seem to have paid full attention to their own sentences. Bringing us up to date on the Dubai Open, a reporter told us that Martina Hingis "overcame some bad moments in the first set, then recovered to beat No. 7 Tamarine Tanasugarn of Thailand in the semifinals." This seems to be setting up a contrast between *overcame* and *recovered*, as if the writer meant to say that Hingis suffered or experienced the bad moments and then recovered from them. But, of course, these two words are on the same side of the fence, with the overcoming creating the recovery. It would have been better, probably, to say that Hingis overcame some bad moments to take the first set and went on to drub Tanasugarn in the second (she won it 6–1).

An NPR report on a horrible accident in Nova Scotia included the sentence: "Four schoolchildren were killed when a bus *lost control*." The bus *went out of control*, as reporters used to take pains to say to avoid any possible charge of libel, but if anyone or anything lost control, it had to be the driver. The bus, after all, was inanimate.

My friend seems almost to have chuckled, however, over a surprising statement in an advertisement bearing the byline of the president of the National Education Association. "Last month," wrote the educator, "we published 'Making Low-Performing Schools a Priority.'" Extreme conservatives have sometimes seemed to accuse the NEA of such anti-intellectual purposes, but one hardly expected to hear agreement from the president of the organization. "Think about what you're saying," my friend likes to say, "and say what you mean."

A little more thought might have kept the Washington football team's publicist from boasting on the organization's Web page that REDSKINS READ CHILDREN'S BOOKS. And further cerebration might have kept a *Washington Post* headline writer (for the on-line edition) from declaring: SALVADORANS LOOK FOR MORE VICTIMS. It wasn't that these Central Americans had suddenly turned bloodthirsty—they were simply trying to find survivors of an earthquake.

Those preparing an ad for a Los Angeles store also could have profited from the advice to think and think again; it might have kept them from producing this blaring headline: SLIP-COVERS—A NEW LOOK FOR MOM. One recipient of the mailer noted, "Somebody has a big mama."

One of the best contributions here came from the popular National Public Radio program *All Things Considered*. Reporting on a widely covered trial, the cohost of the program declared: "A Florida teenager was sentenced today . . . to twenty-eight years in prison for shooting his teacher between the eyes." At the bottom of the memo page the grouch had scribbled, "How many years would the boy have received for shooting the teacher between the toes?" And in a second note he posed an important question: "How's the teacher?" The point, of course, was that the boy was sentenced for killing the teacher, not for shooting the victim in one particular part of the body or another.

Discussing the threat to the development of new performers posed by the repackaging of old recordings of "seminal figures," a record executive declared (in the *New York Times Magazine*): "In very practical terms, if you're not among the *uninitiated*, you go into a store and you are confronted with a decision [on] the complete Monk on Blue Note or the new Eric Reid or Brad Mehldau," and you will, said the executive, pick the seminal figure and thus fail to discover new artists. Surely he meant "if you're not among the *initiated*," and it would have been nice of the editors to have helped him out.

Simple structure constitutes the problem here: "In February, Hong Kong jeweler Lan Sai-wing introduced a solid-gold bathroom (including washbasin and two toilets), constructed as homage to Vladimir Lenin's critique of capitalist waste, telling reporters that he had *dreamed* all his life to *have* enough money to build a gold toilet." If you're going to dream such a dream at all, you dream *of having*, of course.

(I occasionally wondered whether I dared mention to my friend that some people—intellectuals!—write vaguely and cloudily *on purpose!* I was thinking here not of academics in general but of a more specialized group, those who say they must attack language and try to "destabilize" it in order to destroy its "illegitimate" power over all of us. They therefore consider it their noble duty to produce prose that varies between simple sloppiness and absolute unintelligibility. They certainly do not appear to have taken to heart, or even to have heard, George Orwell's observation that "the slovenliness of our language makes it easier for us to have foolish thoughts." But I never could make myself bring up the point. The grouchy grammarian already suffered enough without having to cope with the idea that anybody would deliberately produce bad writing.)

• • •

I conclude this topic with a look at a persistent mental picture. It shows my friend leaning forward in his chair, barking at the TV screen: "As far as the humidity *what?*" He was watching the weather news, and for what I gathered was at least the thousandth time was berating the reporter for treating *as far as* as the equivalent of *as for*. If you say "as far as," he never tires of telling me, you must supply not only a subject but a verb as well: *as far as* the humidity *is concerned, as far as* the plot goes . . .

Think! the grouchy grammarian enjoins us all, friend or foe.

THE GROUCH'S REMINDERS

- Think about what you're saying!
- Pay attention to what a word means and where it came from. If you don't know, look it up.
- Pay attention to the arrangement of words in a sentence.
- *Somewhat* is an adverb; *something* is a noun.
- Be kind to metaphors.
- Don't use old sayings and figures of speech you're only vaguely familiar with. They will only get you into trouble.

Agreement; or, Where Did the Subject Go?

In a discussion of some of Donald Trump's financial whirligigging, a *New York Times* reporter said (or a misguided copy editor caused the reporter to say): "A close reading of the documents he released last week as part of his plan to sell stock in his least troubled gambling casino *throw* a spotlight on the financial tightrope he is walking."

Now we're all supposed to have learned, early in our schooling, that the subject of a sentence and the predicate verb of that sentence must agree; that is, both must be singular or both must be plural. All right, simple enough. Why, then, do we often see a singular subject—*reading*, in the case of the Donald Trump sentence—followed by a plural verb—here, *throw?* The grouchy grammarian suggests two reasons: (1) Those making such mistakes attended elementary and junior high or middle schools that took too many snow days; (2) these persons know the rule—which is, after all, about as simple and logical a rule as could be devised—but don't know how to find and characterize the subject. Sometimes they don't even try, but simply make the verb agree with the nearest noun. (My friend, who believes that subject-verb agreement—which is also known, charmingly, as *concord*—constitutes the first requisite of the harmony a sentence must have, calls this mistake the *fallacy of the nearest noun*.) Can this be true even of reporters and broadcasters—persons who have chosen to live by the word? Yes, unfortunately, it can indeed. An untidily full drawer in the grammarian's study clearly shows this to be the most common error made by journalists, as well as by members of all other occupations.

In the *Times* sentence just quoted, the most likely possibility is that when it came time to insert the verb, the writer couldn't make his way through all the spotlights and tightropes back to the subject. But, to his credit, he didn't simply settle for the nearest noun—here, *casino*—but went back as far as *documents*. Actually, of course, he chose the only noun in this sentence that could pose a problem of agreement for him. Bad luck, perhaps, but inadequate preparation and insufficient concentration as well.

Even in a much shorter sentence a writer can lose his way, as in this one from an AP story on the problems faced by flying schools across the country in the aftermath of the September 2001 terrorist attacks in New York and Washington: "Companies like Wayne Breeden's Helicopters Inc. in Memphis, Tenn., *has* lost $2,000 a day." Obviously the writer focused on the company he named and forgot that it was a specific example illustrating the problems of the class he was actually talking about.

In one of the never-ending stories about life on Mars, the reporter acquitted himself well in a situation only to slip two words later: "Friedmann said that on Earth the bacteria that *make* magnetite *forms* the material in chains and that these chains are surrounded by a membrane." The writer recognized that *bacteria* is plural, but then, inexplicably, switched to the singular for *forms*. Or did the singular and snugly close *magnetite* sway him?

A barrage of nouns apparently influenced a Knight Ridder writer to produce this graphic lack of concord in his discussion of the hearings relating to the confirmation of Gale Norton as secretary of the interior in the second Bush administration.

"[Norton's supporters] said her attackers' list of her conservative positions—including opposition to affirmative action, race-based scholarships, handicapped ramps on public buildings and federal air pollution–law enforcement—were taken out of context." *Positions*, to be sure, is the most likely culprit here.

This sentence from the *New York Times* is a pure classic: "The creation of preclearance [customs] facilities in San Francisco and Anchorage *are* being discussed by officials of the two nations."

And look at this sentence from the *New Yorker:* "A fair accounting of the problems of the office of the independent counsel—the ever expanding scope, length, and cost of its work, and its insistent focus on behavior that may not be criminal at all—*suggest* that these problems owe more to the nature of the law establishing the office than to any particular occupant." Though this sentence presents a structural problem or two of its own, the important point here is that the words set off by the dashes clarify and expand the subject but do not change it; it remains *accounting*.

Or take this sentence in an AP report on new discoveries about the ice ages: "James White, a climatologist at the University of Colorado, Boulder, said that an analysis of new ice cores from Antarctica *show* that the south polar area went through a rapid temperature increase." It doesn't take much more than a microsecond to see that it is the *analysis*, not the cores, that *shows* . . .

A *Times* report from the Kosovo war provided a poignant example of this error: "[S]exual assault and intimidation, if not rape, were widespread, used by Serbian forces to strike at the heart of a Muslim society in which fidelity of women *are* central."

Commenting on the low TV ratings of one year's National Basketball Association finals, an AP writer said that "America's unfamiliarity with [San Antonio] Spurs' stars Tim Duncan and David Robinson *were* also blamed for the fall-off." The writer almost seems to put the blame on the stars themselves rather than on the public's unfamiliarity with them.

Writing a few days after the concluding of the 1998 Israeli-Palestinian Wye River agreement, the columnist William Safire commented: "Now *comes* borders, statehood, security, water, capital city—the hard part." That sentence has a five-part subject, one element of which is itself plural, yet the writer supplied a singular verb (no doubt because it comes before the subject). "Hard part" is best thought of as an appositive, a word or a group of words that immediately follows another word or group of words and means the same thing (just like this very definition).

Reporting on the O. J. Simpson "trial of the century," a network correspondent offered a classic instance of the nearest-noun fallacy when she said that "the chance of crime-scene mistakes *are* greater" because a trainee took part in the investigation.

In a story on a completely different but even more closely watched case, the AP summed up the view of a small-town citizen: "[President] Clinton's handling of the substantive issues, especially the economy, *are* what is important."

During his narration of a J. Edgar Hoover biography on the A&E network, Jack Perkins said of the FBI director that "the legend of his accomplishments and those of his G-men *live* on." But it is the *legend* that is being talked about, and it is this legend that *lives* on. *Accomplishments* and *those* are simply the particular items that make up the legend. In the same way, the small-town citizen was judging Clinton's handling of the issues, not the issues themselves. No mystery in either of these cases, really.

On another A&E program, this one having to do with Orson Welles, the narrator made the same kind of mistake: "His work in other people's projects *were* only a preliminary to his own." Is it really so hard to identify the subject in such a sentence? No, certainly not, says the grouchy grammarian, as long as you're willing to pay even minimal attention to what you're talking about. No doubt subject-verb agreement ought to be so ingrained in us as to seem almost instinctual, but clearly that is often not the case; hence we must work on it.

(At this point, I felt that I had probably chosen enough examples of subject-verb disagreement to make the point clear. When I showed the list to the grouch, however, he demanded more. "This is the area in which mistakes are most common," he said. "I see a hundred of them every day. Perhaps more. You must present a variety of examples to illustrate the kinds of possibilities and drive the point home." And, as I went about my ordinary pursuits during the next few hours, I decided that my friend was right. Just as I was on my way to my keyboard to resume work on this topic, I heard a congressman's assistant, appearing on CNN, try to ward off criticism of his boss [who was involved in a messy personal affair] by saying: "We have to see what the basis of these allegations *are*." During the rest of the day I encountered a good twenty more examples. Hence I cheerfully went back to the overstuffed files.)

An AP story, this one concerning Nielsen ratings, told us that "if a show's ratings go up, so *do* the price of ads." It do? Really? It's the *price*, of course, that *goes* up, not the ads themselves.

Information about Thomas Jefferson and his habits is always interesting. From a *New York Times* wine column we learn that "Jefferson's fascination with wine, including his efforts to grow wine grapes in Virginia, *have* been well documented."

The *Times Literary Supplement* (London) offers us some further interesting information, this of a literary nature: "The best known of the previous biographies . . . is that by Enid Starkie, who carried out much of the documentary scholarship on which our knowledge of Rimbaud's 'lost years' *are* based." (Despite the agreement problem, this sentence has its good points, too, as we'll see in Topic 22.)

An unusually striking instance of concord confusion comes from a book about the great San Francisco earthquake and fire.

Describing the plight of one family trying to flee the scene of disaster, the author tells us that "the mattress, with mother and baby, *were* placed in the wagon."

Do such examples mean that we have raised a generation that is literally incapable of looking at a sentence and, without great reflection, seeing what makes it go—what is being talked about and what this subject is doing? The grouch tends to think so, but in reluctant fairness he produced a remarkably glaring example of subject-verb disagreement that came not from a younger writer but from the veteran Mort Walker, creator of the "Beetle Bailey" comic strip. In a block of prose introducing one strip, Walker said: "It's spring and the sound of birds *are* in the air." The birds may often take to the air, all right, but that isn't what Walker wanted to say—it's the *sound* that he's talking about. *Sound*, of course, *is*, not *are*.

Here's a sentence (spoken on National Public Radio) the grouchy grammarian found particularly irritating: "Opponents say that [Charlton] Heston's support for gun-control laws thirty years ago *show* that he's wishy-washy on gun owners' rights." (It should be "support . . . *shows*," of course.) Shaking his head, my friend muttered something about "these reporters," and went on: "Nobody's ever told them what they ought to say, and they haven't been curious enough to find out for themselves. They just don't have any notion of the organic nature of the sentence." I couldn't argue much with that—even if I'd been foolish enough to try.

Note this striking flub from another NPR program: "An Iraqi lawyer handling the appeal of two imprisoned Americans *say* he will plead their case within a week." Apparently the plural "Americans" was so intimately close that the wire-service writer couldn't resist making the verb plural to match it—and thus succeeded in producing nonsense.

Somewhat more complex is the situation in which you take a close look at the subject and it seems at least a bit plural but actually isn't. Reporting on a group of discontented small-town teenagers, an on-the-spot TV reporter said: "She, like many other kids, *say* there's nothing to do." Actually, the basic sentence is: "She *says* there's nothing to do"; "like many other kids" merely gives us additional information. If, however, the reporter had said: "She *and* many other kids say there's nothing to do," she of course would have been correct. As broadcast, the sentence was structured to give us the opinion of this one teenager, and therefore required a singular verb. If you have any question in such a case, a simple way to check yourself is to rearrange the sentence: "Like many other kids, she says there's nothing to do." The need for the singular verb then becomes obvious.

Rearrangement would have saved an NPR correspondent from a similar error: "He, along with fellow Kurds, *are* living in the South." The sentence requires a plural verb only when the subject is plural—*teenagers, Kurds*—or when *she, he,* or any other singular noun or pronoun is followed by *and*, thus creating a true plural subject.

In this context, a Knight Ridder correspondent quite properly refused to be seduced by *plus* and gave us this correct sentence: "The rise of Microsoft as the dominant company on the electronic desktop, plus its bid to monopolize cyberspace, *suggests* that it could be a more than formidable competitor in the news business." The reporter saw that whatever supplementary information he provided, *rise* remained the subject.

Sometimes, even when a writer has correctly identified the subject, problems remain. The reporter covering a ticket sale who reported that "each of these people *are* paying ten bucks a head" obviously thought that with a crowd around, the plural was called for. But *each* and *every* are both singular—each *one* and every *one*.

The undue influence of numbers also shows up in the kind of sentence you see in newspapers every day, particularly in articles bringing us depressing information about health and medical issues: "One in five school-age children *say* they have tried inhalants at least once in their lives" (Knight Ridder). With millions of youngsters in the picture, the writer seems to feel, surely this sentence demands a plural verb.

The same thinking guided the author of this sentence in the *New Yorker:* "Santiago, the capital city—where one in every three Chileans now *live*—sprawls in a fertile bowl of land beneath the Andean cordillera." But no, in both cases. The first sentence actually breaks down the children into groups of five, and says that in every such group, *one* child *is* at risk; the latter sentence performs a similar division with the Chileans: out of every three Chileans, *one lives* in the capital.

An AP writer, however, produced an unusual reverse in this specific area: "An estimated *four* in 10 Americans *uses* some form of alternative medicine."

Sportswriters frequently make a particular kind of singular-plural mistake while obviously trying to write with strict correctness. They say, for example: "The Yankees had *its* biggest lead in the fourth inning." This, obviously, is not English; no even faintly educated person trying to find out the score of a game would ask, "*Is* the Yankees still leading?" The writer may have thought that since *New York* represents the name of a team—a singular name—then *Yankees*, as an alternative team name, should also be singular. But that isn't the case; *New York* is singular and *Yankees* is plural.

An AP story about the Indians contained the opposite (and much less common) mistake: "Cleveland, which last led the division from June 6–10, *are* 5–2 this season against the Twins."

The *New York Times* gave us the following sentence in its description of a basketball game between Georgia Tech and the University of Cincinnati: "The Yellowjackets also had 27 assists, hit 80 percent of *its* free throws, and all five starters each scored in double figures." My crusty old friend can't tell you why the

Times did that (and, for that matter, neither can I), but we can say that the more you look at that sentence, the more problems you see with it. (You'll meet it again in Topic 28, False Series.) In any case, saying *its* for *their* may well represent too great an effort to be correct, a sort of verbal equivalent of crooking the pinkie to speed tea on its way down your gullet.

In a story dealing with the NCAA basketball tournament, the writer tried to solve the problem by choosing both usages. Discussing Temple University's chances of winning the championship that year, he said: "The Owls (24–13) *weren't* expected to get this far, beating three higher-seeded teams before *their* run ended"—three nice plurals in a row. But when, just two paragraphs later, the reporter came to Michigan State, he turned his coat by saying that "the Spartans reached a goal that seemed improbable after losing stars Mateen Cleaves and Morris Peterson from *its* title team."

Note a special case about which we find a great deal of confusion. Think how many times you've seen a sentence like this one (from *Parade*): "The newest entry in the prepared-foods category *are* fully cooked, refrigerated pot roasts." Here, as everywhere else, the verb should agree with the subject; never mind what comes later (which, in this case, is a predicate nominative). *Entry* is singular and, therefore, the verb should be *is*, not *are*. (But the grouch reminds me that a writer can often improve a sentence by making both subject and predicate nominative either singular or plural—making them, that is, agree with each other, endowing the sentence with concord and harmony.)

As a sort of bonus for my grouchy friend, I list without comment several sentences that demonstrate, in various ways, the continuing—and seemingly almost limitless—need for a bit of concord, the clarity-bestowing agreement between subject and verb. As my friend says, this rule is just about the simplest one that anybody could devise, and when we observe it we are not only showing that we're thinking clearly but, by delivering our ideas to other persons, are helping them think clearly and effectively as well. We do have faith in our own ideas, don't we?

"For pharmaceutical companies, research and development costs are high, but the *cost* of making the pills *are* relatively low." *(New York Times)*

"[In a breach-of-contract lawsuit] the *nature* of Judith Reinsdorf's health problems *weren't* disclosed." (AP)

"The *combination* of Cheney's vast Washington experience—as a White House chief of staff, a leader in the House and a defense secretary—and Bush's inexperience *are* likely to yield the vice president a starring role in charting America's course." (Knight Ridder)

THE GROUCH'S REMINDERS

- The subject and predicate verb of a sentence must agree; that is, both must be singular, or both must be plural.

- Beware the fallacy of the nearest noun!

- If in doubt about whether a subject is plural, try rearranging the sentence: "She, like many other kids, *says* [not *say*] there is nothing to do."

- Don't let numbers confuse the subject-verb issue: "*one* in five" takes a singular verb.

- The verb should agree with the subject, not the predicative nominative: "The newest entry in the prepared-foods category *is* fully cooked, refrigerated pot roasts."

Special Kinds of Subjects {3}

When we hear a remark like "tarring and feathering *are* too good for that sneak," we sense that something is not quite right. At least, if we're the grouchy grammarian, we sense it. But why? Two words serving as nouns are sitting right there in the subject spot, aren't they? Yes, indeed they are, but nevertheless the sentence is telling us about one punishment, not two.

Although the rule of subject-verb agreement, or concord, did not become firmly set until the eighteenth century, it has since, as my grouchy friend says, become the key to clarity for the sentence and thus to true communication. But a mid-twentieth-century grammarian, Margaret Bryant, observed that "good prose of today does not always follow the rule," since one could often find sentences in which a singular verb accompanies a plural subject, such as: "But the assault and robbery *is* at least equally likely to have been a reason for his voluntary resignation."

Well, yes, there are two nouns sitting in the subject spot, but, as Bryant goes on to say, "if a group of words, even though plural in form, creates one conception in the mind of the person using them as a subject, a singular verb follows. In Modern English where there is a conflict between form and meaning, meaning tends to triumph." So, literally, the sentence gives us two

31

nouns in the subject spot, but in fact they simply name one action—indeed, one *the* serves for both nouns; when we have two such nouns linked by *and*, we speak of a compound subject.

The same principle holds in "tarring and feathering *are* too good for that sneak," which should read "*is* too good," and in a sentence like "Rupert decided that dinner and a movie *was* just the ticket," except that this latter sentence involves pleasure rather than punishment.

Speaking of a basketball player who had returned to action after operations on both knees, his coach commented: "Now his mobility and agility *is* back." Clearly the coach saw these traits as blending into one athletic quality. If he had said "*his* mobility and *his* agility," he would have been separating them.

A particularly good example here comes from a speech by Prince Charles, in which, calling for Britons to live in harmony, he observed that nobody has a monopoly on truth and then declared: "To recognize that is, I believe, a first step to real wisdom and a vital blow against the suspicion and misunderstanding that too often *characterizes* the public relationships between different faiths."

The distinction between singular and plural in verb forms has little practical value, no doubt; except for forms of *to be (am, was)*, it occurs only in the present tense and there only in the third person. Nevertheless, it exists and is generally observed in literature (which the grouch is sworn to protect) and in daily life, and failure to use it therefore creates confusion; hence my friend supports and favors it.

Meaning also outranks form, Bryant comments, when we use collective—group—nouns (although, as she does not say, a good deal of individual choice comes into play here). Often we say "the class *were* all present" if we're talking about the behavior of the individuals making up the group. On the other hand, we say "the class *was* ranked first" if we're thinking of it as a unit.

Any reader of British writing will have noticed that the plural commonly appears here, as shown, for instance, in this line from a Winston Churchill memo to his air minister: "The Cabinet *were* distressed to hear from you that you were now running short of pilots for fighters."

Meaning or not, however, a line like that often sounds unnatural to Americans (but in the realm of grammar and usage, Churchill, a great admirer of H. W. Fowler's *Modern English Usage*, always stood on firm national ground). And Americans always say "the government *was*," never "the government *were*."

Whatever your nationality or your inclinations in this area, however, you need to be consistent within a sentence. In reporting the problems encountered in Greece by a group of British and Dutch tourists for engaging in their curious hobby of taking photographs at foreign air-force bases, an AP correspondent said: "The group *was* arrested after the Kalamata show and *have* been held since on espionage charges." Such strong disagreement within a sentence can hardly be considered polite. If the writer, pulled between the singular and the plural, did not wish to make *group* plural, she might well have solved her problem by saying simply, "The *members* of the group were . . ."

THE GROUCH'S REMINDERS

- If the subject has two or more nouns but describes one action ("assault and battery"), use a singular verb.
- Don't be afraid to use a plural verb with a plural idea, even if your subject looks singular ("the class were all present").

A Bit More about *Each*

In commenting on how unusual it was for two unbeaten Southeastern Conference football teams to meet late in the season, an AP sportswriter pointed out: "*Each* team has an identical record—8–0 overall and 5–0 in the conference." The writer has produced a sloppy, uncraftsmanly sentence. As it stands, the sentence is incomplete because *each* is being asked to do a job it cannot do. "Each team has a record of 8–0" would be fine, or, alternatively, the sentence could go on to tell us something like this: "Each team has a record identical to that of the great Georgia Tech team of 1887," or whatever it might be. Why? Because *identical* must be identical to something; it can't float. There isn't much mystery here about what the writer means—the two teams have identical records—but the point has been blunted.

Sometimes a writer simply doesn't give us *each* when we may need it. Discussing the out-of-court settlement of a lawsuit over a "sex tape" made by Pamela Anderson and a rock singer named Brett Michaels, an entertainment column noted that "Internet Entertainment Group agreed to pay *both* participants a seven-figure sum and destroy all copies." This decision probably did not result in any great loss to art, but it's cloudy in one respect: Is Internet Entertainment paying Anderson and Michaels *each* a seven-figure sum, or is that the grand total? If it's the latter, then the writer would have been well advised to say so explicitly, because *both* is commonly and confusingly used where *each* is actually called for.

This sentence (from *American Profile*) is typical: "At *both* ends of the elliptical design [of the planned World War II memorial in Washington] will stand a towering baldachin, or canopy—one representing the Atlantic theater, the other the Pacific." Quite a mobile canopy!

In describing the successes achieved by two operas at the festival in Aix-en-Provence, a *New York Times* critic commented: "It no doubt helped that *each* came with excellent productions." But *each* is still one, and therefore each came with *an* excellent *production*.

THE GROUCH'S REMINDER

Each is always singular. Use *both* when you mean both.

There—the Introducer {5}

A writer who wants the verb to precede instead of follow the subject of a sentence can easily arrange it, because nature has supplied a handy introductory word: *there*. "There *is* a Boy Scout on every corner" and "There *are* Boy Scouts everywhere."

But what do we often hear? We hear sentences like this: "*There's* Boy Scouts everywhere." *Boy Scouts* is the subject—the unmistakably plural subject—yet throughout the media, and also in the great world outside, speakers will give it a singular verb. The grouchy grammarian fears that many of these writers and speakers see *there* as the subject, precisely because it comes before the verb, even though it's only a doorman, a function word (once called an introductory adverb) to get you into the sentence. He believes that's probably the case, for instance, with Robert Putnam, the Harvard sociologist who wrote *Bowling Alone*, the much-discussed analysis of threats to community in America. Speaking of the need to preserve groups like the League of Women Voters, Putnam said that newer advocacy groups may be popular but do not fill the void: "There's a lot of smoke there; *there's* a lot of mirrors there. But there's not something that has yet replaced it." (*There's* Nos. 1 and 3 are, of course, correct.)

In an interview on CNN, President George W. Bush, who

like all presidents belongs in the category of media figure by virtue of the office he holds and hence is subject to being quoted in these pages, displayed a similar fondness for this construction: "If *there's* any environmental regulations *that's* preventing California from having a 100 percent max output at their plants . . . then we need to relax those regulations." (*That's*, instead of *that are*, represents a kind of bonus here.)

Speaking of Rick Pitino, the renowned basketball coach who appears in this book several times (if not as frequently as he pops up in the national press) and who was weighing an offer from a university, the broadcaster Dick Vitale observed, "He's going to coach in college. *There's* no ifs, ands or buts about it." (Vitale proved to be an accurate prophet.)

A less obvious and therefore quite useful example comes from an AP story about the need for former presidents of the United States to speak with care when they visit foreign countries: "[Lee] Hamilton, a former chairman of the House International Relations Committee, said he is not in favor of a 'gag rule' but *there needs* to be clear lines of communication between former and sitting chief executives." *Lines*, not *there*, is the subject here; as noted above, *there* is never the subject.

Using the contraction *there's* instead of saying *there is* probably makes this error a bit more attractive to users but doesn't change its nature—*'s* is still singular—and if you have a plural subject, you need a plural verb, my friend harrumphs. He would be ashamed, he rumbled, to be fooled by the presence of *there*.

Beyond that, he pointed out, a writer should use the introductory *there* sparingly. With a grimace intended, I believe, as a smile, he allowed himself a joke: "You know, Parrish, *there's* better ways to build a sentence." Then, perhaps less lightly, he added: "As you do your writing, you might note this point yourself." His sense of humor, I'm afraid, does not stretch as far as I sometimes might wish.

THE GROUCH'S REMINDER

There is an introductory adverb, never the subject of a sentence. The verb still agrees with the subject, even if it comes afterward.

Former Greats {6}

One snowy February evening I heard an NPR broadcaster explain that the Presidents' Day holiday honors "former President Washington and former President Lincoln."

I later noted among the grouch's clippings a photo caption that spoke of "former President Franklin D. Roosevelt."

In Henry Kissinger's book *Diplomacy*, similarly, the caption of a World War I photo of the Kaiser with his generals speaks of "former Emperor William II."

But saying "former President Washington" or "former President Roosevelt" makes about as much sense as saying "former King Tut." After January 20, 2001, we spoke of "former President Clinton" to distinguish this very-much-alive worthy from his successor in the office; *former* conveys the idea that Clinton once was president and then turned to other pursuits. After a person's death, however, the need for such a distinction disappears, whether or not the particular government continues to exist: Washington and Wilhelm are president and Kaiser forever, just as Victoria is eternally a queen and David eternally a king. (If the president's or other official's time of service had been relatively recent, it would be helpful to give the dates, and you can, of course, provide any other needed information.)

Besides that, as the grouch pointed out one day, to speak of "former Emperor William II" with reference to a 1917 photograph could easily mislead the reader, inasmuch as the Kaiser did indeed live on for many years during which he was truly "former," but that has-been period didn't begin until November 1918.

Since Lincoln and Roosevelt both died in office, neither even in his own lifetime ever had the status of former president. A bonus point here: Alex Trebek, the host of the TV program *Jeopardy*, referred to Jefferson Davis as "the former president of the Confederacy," even though no conceivable confusion exists in this case, since no other person has ever held that particular office or ever will hold it.

In a news story on the establishment of a minor-league baseball team in a southwestern Pennsylvania town, the AP noted that the team's nickname—the Generals—honored prominent generals from the area, among them George C. Marshall, "a *former* secretary of state and chairman of the Joint Chiefs of Staff." Wrong on both counts. Marshall, who has been dead since 1959, is not among us to be confused by anyone with a current holder of the State portfolio (it would be better to say when he served), and he was chief of staff of the army, not chairman of the Joint Chiefs (a position that did not come into existence until after Marshall's time of active service).

A classic straining of *former* occurs in this obituary of a noted architect and college dean, who is described as having "served as *former* president of the Kentucky State Board of Examiners and Registration of Architects." The man did no such thing, of course—he served as president of the board. Serving as *former* president would hardly have given him much to do. If his dates of service were for some reason not available, the reporter could have solved his problem by saying that the dean *had served* as president of the board.

"Try to keep it simple, Parrish," my grouchy friend told me. "Keep your eye on all these petty pedants who think they're promoting accuracy when they do things like this. These are just a few examples, you know—just specimens. You must look sharp and catch miscreants in the act when they're blowing this kind of smoke. And remind your readers that sometimes just an additional word or two can make everything clear."

One day some time later, glancing through a small-town newspaper, I came across what must be the ultimate example of *former* smoke-blowing. An obituary notice described the deceased person as a "former native" of the town. If you were born there, of course, you cannot be unborn. I don't think you can pursue *former* much beyond that, although a different newspaper offered an interesting parallel when it characterized a deceased academic as a "former professor emeritus." I wondered what the poor fellow could possibly have done during his retirement to cause him to lose his doubtless hard-earned badge of merit.

THE GROUCH'S REMINDER

Use *former* only to describe people still living (*former* President Clinton, not *former* President Washington.)

Just Because They Sound Alike . . . {7}

My old friend was usually irritated but sometimes amused when writers fell for soundalikes (or near soundalikes), as one small-town newspaper feature writer did with these two beauties: she spoke of someone's curiosity as having been *peaked* and described a cuisine as *hardy*. In general, it seems, the smaller the newspaper, the more exotic the errors it commits. But, as the grouch reminds me, we're not shooting at small-town papers—certainly not when big game abounds.

The "sounds alike" trap can be persuasive and sinister, indeed. The *New Yorker* offered this thoughtful but flawed sentence: "Chile's vaunted economic miracle was brought about by the so-called Chicago Boys, a group of Chilean disciples of the American economist Milton Friedman, who were given free *reign* to put their theories into practice." But the metaphor here has to do with horses, not monarchs. *To give free rein* is, of course, to abandon restraint, just as *to take the reins* is to assume control. (As my friend says, "free reign," having no meaning at all, represents a clear and cautionary example of metaphor abuse.)

Similar but even more common is this spelling switch: "Watching the dissection of President Clinton's private life cannot be a very encouraging sight for 52-year-old [George W.]

Bush, even though he has apparently followed the *straight* and narrow for a good 10 years now" (Froma Harrop, syndicated columnist). The expression does not mean linear as well as narrow but goes back to the Gospel of St. Matthew: "*Strait* is the gate, and narrow is the way"; both adjectives mean narrow. A famous nineteenth-century example comes from the William Ernest Henley poem "Invictus": "It matters not how *strait* the gate . . ." As a noun, the word is universally familiar in the names of tight geographical squeezes: *Strait* of Gibraltar.

In an interview with Ann Landers, a *New York Times* reporter assured us that Ann "hordes typewriter ribbons in a closet in case they become unobtainable." *Hordes?* Perhaps the interviewer was thinking that hordes of ribbons make a *hoard*—and perhaps not. The verb here should be *hoards*, just as it should be *hoard* in the following case. Discussing one of the many twists and turns in the battle over contraception and abortion, the *Lexington Herald-Leader* offered the sprightly comment that antiabortion activists were apparently "afraid women will *horde* their oral contraceptives and pop several after sex to prevent any fertilized egg from implanting in the uterus."

While offering advice to job seekers, the *Chicago Tribune* provided an instance of an extremely common error: "In most cases, you can *diffuse* the insulting comments and questions." But why would somebody who is unemployed wish to go around spreading—*diffusing*—insults in the hearing of prospective employers? (My grumpy friend might do something of the kind, but that's a different story.) *Defuse*, a verb coined for World War II bomb squads, is the word needed here.

A mail-order catalogue offers what is apparently a flattering item: its "16" halogen Brushed Steel Dome Lamp is the perfect *compliment* to any exquisite desk set." If you trace the origins of *compliment* and *complement* back far enough, you will come to the Latin word meaning *complete*. But that's pretty far back. In practice, to *complement* still means to fill out or complete; to *compliment* is to express admiration or esteem.

In a book advertisement that appeared in the *New Republic*, Penguin Books declared that "*Beyond Machiavelli* was originally drafted by Roger Fisher, the *principle* author of the worldwide bestseller *Getting to Yes*." The writer means *principal*, which can be either an adjective (as it would be here) or a noun (high school *principal*, the *principals* in a business deal); *principle* (a doctrine, law, or code) is never anything but a noun. The reverse mistake appears in this AP story about an astronomer's search for fellow creatures in the universe: "Although Drake found no evidence of extraterrestrial life, ongoing research elsewhere uses the *principals* he established."

A monthly bill from a cellular-phone company claims that with a battery charger that plugs into your car's cigarette lighter, you can have "the *piece-of-mind* that your family has a communications link in case of emergency." And, to be sure, you can give them a piece of your mind if they don't use it. "*Peace of mind*" is what the company meant to say. In any case, *peace* to all parties. (And with cigarette lighters serving for everything but lighting cigarettes, it may be time to give them a more up-to-date name.)

This one is positively evil: A certain state senator "received the chairmanship of the Labor and Industry Committee, which pleased the former tool and dye maker." As a specialized kind of tool, *die* was needed here, but perhaps in his industrial career the delighted senator had turned out some colorful tools.

With altogether unbecoming glee, the grouch cited this example from the *New York Times*: "[Dale Carnegie Training] became a *right* of passage for young executives who sought to develop the confidence to present themselves well in public settings." (Of course, a defender of this sentence might say that the Carnegie *rite* became a right.) With equal delight, my friend quoted another sentence from the *Times*: "Unlike her contemporary Robert Gober, who regularly produces *discreet* objects as well as full installations, until recently [Ann] Hamilton has worked only with complex tableaux." The scrambling of *rite* (a ceremony) and *right* (something to which one is entitled) and discrete (separate; not connected) and *discreet* (prudent; capable of keeping a secret) suggests undue reliance on the computer spelling checker, a useful but intellectually limited tool. It also suggested to the grouchy grammarian that the writers and editors should have been capable of outwitting the checker.

Perhaps the most notable item here comes from a clipping, unfortunately undated but yellowed enough to show that the grouch ripped it from his newspaper quite a few years ago, announcing the definitive end of a much covered political-cinematic romance: "Now that actress Debra Winger and actor Timothy Hutton are married, Nebraska Gov. Bob Kerrey will forever hold his *piece*." No comment seems needed.

The old grouch would like me to call *piece-peace* and all other such word pairs *homophones*—and he would even settle for *homonyms*—but I fear that in using such terms I would run the risk of alienating readers who might benefit from our help. Like everybody else, my friend hears all the talk about dumbing-down in schools. In fact, he will admit—if you press (not *pressure*) him—that the process had already begun in his own school days. Educators in that distant era already spoke not of *declensions* of Latin nouns, for instance, but of the homier-sounding *families;* and *be, seem, feel,* and other such *copulative* verbs had given up their licentious ways and dwindled into asexual *linking* verbs.

No sensible person would try to give here all the misused words, soundalike blunders and similar errors, not even all those from the old grammarian's files. This topic must serve as a snare for your attention and a stimulus to your thought. But we can't resist one more: According to *TV Guide*, NBC likes to use its "most successful shows as *lynchpin* sitcoms." But really, *TV Guide*, would an old hanging judge devote any of his attention to something as small as a pin? (Much to the grouch's disgust, this version of *linchpin* has recently battered its way into respectability in at least one dictionary.)

"I would never have thought of this," the grouch had scribbled on one clipping of recent vintage. In describing a deadly shark attack on a man and woman swimming off the North Carolina shore, a doctor at a nearby medical center said (as noted by a reporter who may not have had much of a gift for spelling): The couple suffered "multiple dramatic" injuries to their legs and buttocks. *Traumatic* (one of today's most popular words), perhaps?

That certainly isn't a typical soundalike case, but if you're a student of words you must always be on the alert for the completely unexpected.

THE GROUCH'S REMINDER

Many words sound like other words. When you're writing, therefore, you need to know just which word you mean.

The *Reason*
Isn't *Because* ...   { 8 }

I n a distinctly less-than-favorable notice of a new Metropolitan Opera production of *Il Trovatore*, the *New York
Times* reviewer observed that "surely the main *reason* the audience reacted so negatively on opening night was *because* they felt
in solidarity with the visibly uncomfortable singers."

Switching to sports, we encounter the same construction.
"The *reason why* the Pacers game was so high [in the TV rat-
ings]," said an AP writer discussing National Basketball Association playoffs, "is primarily *because* it was only watched in the
two host cities and Chicago." This gives us a nice double redundancy: *reason* is reason all by itself, without *why*, and then we
have the reason why is *because*. Omitting the first three words
and *is* would give us a respectable if not graceful sentence: "The
Pacers game was so high primarily because it was only watched
in the two host cities and Chicago." (We might switch *only* and
watched, too.) Or we can keep *reason* and drop *because*: "The reason the Pacers game was so high is primarily that it was . . ."

Similar tidying-up would help the sentence from the *Times*
review; simply remove *because* and replace it with *that*.

The point, of course, is that *because* contains the idea of
reason—it means "for the reason that." One reason per cause

ought to be sufficient. As my grouchy friend says, "It may not be a sin—*may* not be—to say 'the reason is because' and to make some of the other mistakes you're dealing with, but it's weak and it's watery and it harms the language. Be sure to point that out."

May and *Might:* Did They or Didn't They?

For some reason, reporters, broadcasters, and people generally have progressively assigned to the word *may* much of the work that *might* has long and faithfully performed. This change has tended to blur a highly useful distinction and to produce confusion and doubt where we need clarity. In other words, many contemporary sentences with *may* in them don't make sense.

Let us set the stage with two examples from the grouchy grammarian's ample supply: (1) In a note to "Chromedome" (a reader who made jokes about his own baldness), Dear Abby commented drily that "had you found yourself permanently bald at age 21, you *may* not have been able to see the humor in baldness." (2) From State College, Pennsylvania, a basketball writer fiercely loyal to the home team informed us that "if not for one of the worst calls in Penn State history, Indiana *may* have been knocked from its No. 1 ranking."

Now we must ask two questions: Was Indiana knocked from its No.1 ranking? Did Chromedome lose all his hair at age twenty-one? No, in both cases. The terrible call saved the Hoosiers, and Chromedome did not become bald till later. But, amid this stylistic murk, how could a reader be sure just what the writer meant? (For his part, the grouch had drawn heavy black circles around the two *mays*.)

Abby and the sportswriter both needed to say *might*, not *may*. *May* refers to a probability or a possibility that still exists (We *may* see a landing on Mars within twenty years), whereas *might*, in this context, refers to a probability or a possibility that existed in the past but did not materialize (If we had spent 3 trillion dollars on the space program, we *might* have seen a Mars landing by now). Think of *might* here as merely the past tense of *may*.

If you had any question, you can now see why the grouch gets upset at announcers who tell him that "if the runner had slid, he *may* have been safe." My friend "damn well" knows that the runner was not safe, and he thinks the broadcaster ought to know it, too.

I found quite puzzling, in this context, an item in a column in *Parade* by Marilyn Vos Savant, who is famous for her measurements—not of her physical attributes (although she appears to be an extremely attractive person) but of her intellectual qualities (she is said to have the highest known IQ). In this instance, however, she seemed to need help. In answer to a reader's question about the possibility of a woman's having identical triplets, the columnist, after informing the reader that this is indeed possible, states: "For example, all five of the Dionne quintuplets (born in Canada in 1934) were identical. But a different set of quintuplets *may* have developed from one, two, three, four or five fertilized eggs, producing a mix of identical and fraternal siblings." Did Vos Savant mean to tell us that perhaps another set of quints had mysteriously grown up, partly identical, partly fraternal? No, she certainly did not. She meant that another, differing set *might* have developed.

To look at this point in another way: *may* goes with *can*, and *might* goes with *could*. A *Philadelphia Inquirer* columnist neatly scrambled these in this fashion: "If a candidate could present the facts succinctly, Americans *may* be ready to hear some truths." (This sentence really needs redemption; the writer means to say that if the candidate *can* present the facts succinctly, he or she *may discover* that Americans *are* ready to hear some truth; this readiness itself certainly does not depend on the candidate's ability or lack of ability to present the facts succinctly.)

One other set of *may-might* meanings deserves discussion here. When we say "I *may* go to Boston tomorrow," we are not merely expressing a possibility; we're saying that tomorrow quite likely will see us on the way to Boston. If we say that we *might* win the lottery, we're acknowledging a possibility (after all, we bought a ticket) but are realistically expressing a high degree of doubt about it. Thus, if we say that we *might* go to Boston, we're saying that it could happen but there's not much chance of it. *May* expresses a good probability, *might* implies a long shot.

These same degrees of probability apply when the sentences are questions. When you answer a knock at the door and the lady standing there says, "*May* I come in?" she is presuming that the two of you are friends and is expecting to be admitted. If the caller diffidently says, "*Might* I come in?" she either doesn't know you or thinks you're likely to turn her down for some other reason. She may even feel the need to offer some justification for having made such an unorthodox request (heavy rain, snow, pursuit by a threatening person, or some other difficulty).

Of course, your visitor may never have heard of the grouchy grammarian and may say whatever first comes into her head. Then you have a decision to make.

THE GROUCH'S REMINDERS

- *May* refers to a probability or a possibility that still exists, whereas *might* refers to a probability or a possibility that existed in the past but did not materialize.

- *May* goes with *can*, and *might* goes with *could*: "If a candidate *could* present the facts succinctly, Americans *might* [not *may*] be ready to hear some truths."

- In the present tense, use *may* to express a probability ("I *may* go to Boston tomorrow"); use *might* to express doubt about a possibility ("I *might* go to Boston tomorrow.")

As of Yet {10}

Years ago, William Strunk and E. B. White, in the famous little book *The Elements of Style* (written by Strunk, revived and revised by White), pointed out the silliness of saying *as yet* instead of simply *yet*. Neither writer, I'm sure, ever imagined that *as yet* not only would survive and flourish but would give rise to an inflated form: *as of yet*. Say simply "We don't *yet* have any word on Johnson's injuries" instead of "We don't have any word on Johnson's injuries, *as of yet*." What is *as of yet* grammatically? The grouchy grammarian supplied a simple answer: "Who can say?"

Floaters and Danglers

A modifying phrase dangles when it's supposed to tell us about one subject but appears to belong to another subject or to none at all. Though "dangling modifier" has long been a familiar term here, my friend prefers to call all such phrases, whatever form they take, "floaters," because, he says, they don't seem to have any attachment at all to the sentence—they just sail along on their own.

From an insurance company commercial: "As parents, our children depend on us." I don't mean to seem grouchy myself (maybe a little of it rubs off), but if you don't immediately see what's wrong with the quoted sentence, perhaps you should think about finding a nonverbal hobby. The phrase "as parents" must be followed by a statement about these parents ("as parents, we must realize that our children depend on us"), not about some other group, even such a close group as the one made up of darling children.

An obituary, in speaking of the deceased, tells us that "her heart had been weakened *after being treated for lung cancer*." It was the lady, of course, who had undergone the treatments, not her heart. The sentence could better have said, "*After being treated for lung cancer*, she experienced heart complications," so that the modifying phrase would modify *she*, as it should.

Going further afield, let us take note of the flap copy for a British publisher's book on Cold War intelligence: "*Born* in Moscow in 1947, Vladimir Kuzichkin's rapid *promotion* within the ranks of the KGB had marked him down for even higher honours before he decided to seek asylum in the West in 1982." Fascinating stuff, to be sure, but, even so, the publisher cannot convince us that Kuzichkin's *promotion* was born in 1947; Kuzichkin himself was actually the beneficiary of this happy event.

Two other examples concerning personal origins come from the weekly newspaper supplement *American Profile:* "*Born* in Sydney, Australia, Jamie O'Neal's *family* moved to Las Vegas when she was 7" and "*Born* in Sylvania, Ohio, in 1920, Roger Durbin's *pride* in his fellow veterans was nurtured as a tank mechanic in the famed 10th Armored Division."

The Associated Press gave us this comment about Bobby Cox, the veteran manager of the Atlanta Braves: "As the *manager* of the first team in major league history to make six straight postseason appearances, the *glare* of the spotlight is often blinding." Cox, of course, is no more a *glare* than Kuzichkin is a *promotion* or Jamie O'Neal a *family* or Roger Durbin a *pride*; each is, instead, a human being.

More exotic than any of these is this characterization from a ballet review in the *New York Times:* "'Wien,' rightly acclaimed after Mr. Rioult created it in 1995, uses Ravel's first title for 'La Valse.' Often *considered* a neo-Romantic *score*, Mr. Rioult has heard its anti-Romantic dissonance." We definitely agree with Rioult's musical judgment here, but we must point out that, for all his talent and skill, he is not a *score* of any kind but is a choreographer and dancer.

We also have this sentence from a sports column: "Despite [having] just one year of high school experience on his résumé, Kidd was one of only a few coaches willing to give Jackson a crack at playing college football." Did *Kidd*, a college coach, really have only one year of high school experience? No, of course not; *Jackson* obviously was the fellow with the limited high school career. The quoted sentence presents various problems, including the omission of the participle *having*, but let's focus here on role of the whole floating phrase *(Despite just one year . . . on his résumé)*. If the writer had followed this phrase with a statement about Jackson—something like "Jackson had a crack at playing college football"—then the modifier would not drift but would be securely hooked to the rest of the sentence and we would know just what the writer wanted to tell us.

Sometimes, however, a modifier doesn't seem to be attached to anything, as in this sentence from an AP account of a Kentucky-Vanderbilt basketball game: "*Down 58–43*, a 13–0 run—which included a four-point play and a five-point play over a 42-second span—pulled the Commodores within 58–56 with 9:05 remaining." Of course, it was the *Commodores* who were down 58–43, and the sentence can easily be repaired to say so: "Down 58–43, the Commodores produced a 13–0 run . . ."

What particularly seems to invite floating and dangling is the present participle, so much so that almost everybody has heard the term "dangling participle." This sentence from the *Reader's Digest* presents a prime example: "While visiting my five-months-pregnant sister-in-law in Florida, *we* went to her favorite restaurant. The waitress asked Suzie when she was due." This seems to make pregnant Suzie capable of visiting herself. As the sentence is written, *visiting* can only modify *we*, and Suzie is part of the *we*.

In short, a dangler needs to find a hook or, as the grouch would rather say, a floater must have a mooring.

THE GROUCH'S REMINDERS

- A modifying phrase dangles—or floats—when it is supposed to tell us about one subject but appears to belong to another subject or to none at all.

- Present participles are particularly susceptible to dangling. Beware of sentences like this one: "*Having* just one year of high school experience, the coach gave Jackson a crack at playing college football."

A.M./Morning, P.M./Afternoon, Evening {12}

How many times have you heard radio voices telling you that some event will take place at "ten A.M. tomorrow morning"? The logical conclusion to draw from such a statement is either that the broadcaster isn't paying any attention to what he is saying or that he doesn't know what *A.M.* means—because, of course, if it's *A.M.* it cannot be afternoon or evening; it has to be morning. Say either *A.M.* or (preferably) *morning*, but not both. Some of the popularity of *A.M.* and *P.M.* probably comes from the vaguely scientific flavor they can impart to a sentence, whether or not the sentence has any reason to sound scientific. If you want to say *A.M.* or *P.M.*, all right, but leave it at that.

The whole idea of day and night has created other problems, especially for newscasters who work the graveyard shift. Late one evening several years ago, as I drove along an interstate highway, I listened to the last two or three innings of a baseball game between Cincinnati and Pittsburgh. Perhaps ten minutes after it was over, an announcer informed all of us listeners that it was now twelve o'clock. In the ensuing news summary, which included a roundup of baseball scores, the announcer declared that "last night the Pirates defeated the Reds six to five." That surprised me, because the score of the game I had just heard was 6–5. The same score two nights in a row? Well, certainly not impossible. But then the announcer described how the Pirates had come from behind to score three runs in the ninth inning. I had just listened to that rally—he was speaking of events that had taken place only twenty minutes before as having occurred "last night."

When I happened to mention this incident during my next visit to the grouchy grammarian, his face lit up with the kind of negative delight he sometimes takes in contemplating questions of usage and style. "Yes, yes," he said, "that trend just swept in on us from somewhere. California, maybe, like hugging. You see what that broadcaster was doing, don't you?" I thought I did, indeed. Underlying what the newscaster had said was a confusion of two definitions of *day:* (1) the twenty-four-hour period from 12:00 midnight to 12:00 midnight; (2) the part of this twenty-four-hour period when the sun shines (or would if not masked by clouds). *Night*, a nontechnical, visual rather than calendrical concept, includes parts of two calendar days. Reports of military operations therefore speak, for example, of "the mammoth air raid upon Cologne on the night of May 30–31" (Winston Churchill); the U.S. Air Force style manual calls for use of two numbers separated by a slash mark ("the night of *19/20* March") specifically to indicate a night event.

The ball game whose conclusion I heard before midnight and the news report after midnight were thus events of the same night (as, indeed, the word *midnight* itself suggests); the fact that, technically, the game took place on one day and the report was given on another was irrelevant. It would have been a further absurdity to speak of the game as having occurred "yesterday." Even funnier would have been the announcer's problem if the game had gone into extra innings. Would he have told us that the game began "last night" and was continuing "tonight"?

"A fairly creditable summary, Parrish," said my friend (for him, such limited praise amounted to backslapping effusiveness). "The fellow on the radio was trying for precision, fell into ill-informed pedantry, and produced absolute nonsense. Unfortunately, that's not uncommon." He then went on to tell me that once, in his younger and far more social days, he had taken it upon himself to divide the day into its proper stages: morning, from arising till lunch; afternoon, lunch through cocktail time; evening, dinner till bedtime; night, from retiring till arising. But never once, he insisted, had he claimed that this breakdown should have calendrical force.

THE GROUCH'S REMINDER

If you can tell day from night, you'll be ahead of many persons you meet.

Would Have vs. *Had* {13}

I f Gant *would have* caught the ball, the Phillies would have won the game." How often have you heard sentences like that one? To the grouchy grammarian's great distress, they seem to be appearing with increasing frequency. An experienced and thoroughly dedicated outfielder, Ron Gant no doubt wanted to catch that ball (although the speaker suggests, most unfairly, that he *would* not—that is, *did not want to*), but simply was unable to reach it. We need here just the past perfect: "If Gant *had caught* the ball . . ." Do we have any hope of stopping this twisted conditional trend? My old friend earnestly hopes so.

Sports announcers have also created another and quite distinctive conditional, contrary-to-fact form: "If Gant *catches* that ball, the Phillies win the game." There's no real suspense here— Gant has already *not* caught that ball, and the Phillies have already lost the game. This form seems to represent an attempt to create a conditional counterpart of the indicative historical present ("President Lincoln walks over to his desk and slowly lowers himself into his chair"). Color commentators, the sidekicks of the play-by-play broadcasters, seem particularly fond of it, perhaps because they feel that it prolongs the drama, keeping Gant chasing the ball in a sort of verbal instant replay.

TV talk-show hosts play this game, too. Here's Rosie O'Donnell commenting on the possible evils of Jerry Springer's program: "If his show *is* on at night, I don't have a problem with it." But, alas, the program appears during the day, when it's "dangerous for kids." (If Springer's show *were* on at night, it wouldn't be any better, for kids or anybody else, but Rosie wouldn't have needed to use a subjunctive in her sentence.)

THE GROUCH'S REMINDER

Use the right form of the subjunctive in contrary-to-fact conditional sentences. Speaking about the past (even if it's just a minute ago), we say, "If Gant *had* [not *would have*] caught the ball, the Phillies would have won the game." Speaking about the present, we say, "If his show *were* [not *is*] on at night, I *wouldn't* [not *don't*] have a problem with it."

Apostrophe Atrocities {14}

T he grouchy grammarian remarked one day that he could write an encyclopedia about the age-old indignities and perversions to which the poor little apostrophe has been subjected. Three general types of problems plague this innocent bit of punctuation: (1) it is used when it is not needed; (2) it is left out when it is needed; (3) it is needed but is inserted in the wrong place.

"[The rain] always takes me back to sleeping in the upstairs room at my *grandparent's* house," says a nostalgic lady in an advertisement appearing in the *Reader's Digest*. Is she speaking of sweet old Grandma or dear old Granddad? Well, obviously, she's trying to include both grandparents in the ownership of the house and thinks she has done it; whoever edited the ad apparently agreed with her. But what did she actually do? She made perhaps the most common of all the mistakes in punctuation that disfigure published prose (including prose that appears on TV screens and computer monitors). She violated the simple, fundamental, and inflexible commonsense guide to turning a plural noun ending in *s* into a possessive: *Never* split a word apart to insert your apostrophe. Thus, if you're speaking of grandparents, you simply tack on the apostrophe, turning the word into *grandparents'*. Indeed, you never split any other word apart to make it possessive, either; the possessive of Jones, for instance, is *Jones's*, not *Jone's*. Because Jones is a name, the general practice is to add an *s* after the apostrophe.

But here confusion sometimes arises, as in this example from the historian Robert Nisbet's book *Roosevelt and Stalin*, which quotes FDR's adviser Harry Hopkins as saying that the second front in Europe "would constitute [the *Americans's*] major effort." The interpolation in brackets, intended by the editors to make Hopkins's subject plain to the reader, follows the wrong model. It isn't a personal name ending in *s*, like Jones, but a noun that has an *s* because it's a plural, just like grandparents; it needs no further *s* after the apostrophe. This is a classic example of helpfulness that actually turns the reader's attention away from the subject.

In speaking of the *Reader's Digest*, incidentally, one should not be led astray by the trickiness of its name. When DeWitt and Lila Wallace started the magazine back in the 1920s, they apparently envisioned an ideal consumer—the *reader*, a single person sitting in an armchair, engaged in an individual and not a group activity—and thus named their creation for this lone reader, rather than for the masses of subscribers they hoped to attract. Hence the singular noun *reader* is made possessive by the addition of an apostrophe and an *s*.

The following assertion, however, obviously calls for the plural, not the singular: "George Flint, head of the Nevada Brothel *Owner's* Association, thinks the Viagra claims are all hype" (Associated Press). No one would suppose that, however well or poorly Viagra may work, Nevada has only one brothel or one owner, and this benevolent association surely is not an armchair affair with just one member.

Though he's not from Brooklyn, the gruff old grammarian recently felt a bit of nostalgia of his own when he saw a reference to the old Dodger ballpark: *Ebbet's* Field. In this case the author had created a possessive situation where none existed (and, in the bargain, had put the apostrophe in the wrong place—the park got its name from Charles Ebbets). In the old days before corporate billboarding, baseball stadiums and other such entities often bore the proprietor's name, and in unadorned form: Wrigley Field, Briggs Stadium. (That tempting final *s* in "Briggs" should not lure anyone into thinking it any more possessive than Ebbets.)

Even if "Ebbets" were possessive, however, it would not carry an apostrophe; the common practice with institutions, enterprises, associations, and publications is to drop the apostrophe: teachers college, *Publishers Weekly*.

A concert reviewer described the Trio for Clarinet, Cello, and Piano in A Minor (Op. 114) as "music of *Brahm's* maturity, one of the last works completed after he had announced his retirement" *(Sarasota Herald Tribune)*. To be fair about it, I must tell you that this same paragraph also had the correct *Brahms's*—which only shows us how readily writers, editors, and anybody else who works in the print media fall into this error.

In discussing the appointment of Karen Hughes as counselor to President George W. Bush, the AP quoted the views of another Texan, Chuck McDonald, "who was former Gov. Ann *Richard's* spokesman in 1994 when she lost to Bush." Well, *Brahms* is *Brahms* and *Richards* is *Richards*; you can add to them, but nothing can legitimately split them up.

Worse (in view of its subject) than any of these blunders is a guide to literary sites in London that, most unthinkably, directs the reader to *Keat's* house (a London map makes the same mistake).

In a nice switch in the name game, a sign that used to stand outside the California ranch owned by Ronald and Nancy Reagan read: The *Reagan's*. If it had said simply the *Reagans*, it would have been telling us that multiple Reagans lived there; if it had said the *Reagans'*, it would have meant that multiple Reagans owned the place. As it was, it told us nothing that's very clear, because an apostrophe is not used with a name or any other ordinary word to make it plural; the *s* itself does the job.

This point escaped the notice of the person who, in an advertisement for a program designed to combat anxiety and depression, declared that "*medication's* are not the long-term answer."

In Donald E. Westlake's novel *A Likely Story*—a book about a writer that, for any writer who reads it, will produce a mixture of laughter and rueful tears—the copyediting staff produced this surprise: "Yesterday," the hero tells us, "I took the boys . . . to the *Met's* opener out at Shea." If the executives of the Metropolitan Opera—the Met—had decided, for some reason, to open the season in a baseball park, then that statement would have been correct, if a bit slangy. But the New York Mets are a different matter. As a plural, "Mets" already has an *s*; hence, in accordance with the basic principle, we don't split the word apart but simply add the apostrophe after the *s*: *Mets'*. (The grouchy grammarian will grudgingly allow you to follow a current practice in which such a name is treated as an adjective and the apostrophe is omitted. Where people have customarily said, for instance, *Tiger shortstop*, you will now often see *Tigers shortstop*. My friend does not see what the world has gained by this development, but he feels that I should point it out.)

USA Weekend took its own flyer into parenthetical sports by describing the broadcaster Jim Nantz as overwhelmingly busy covering "basketball's 'March madness' and the *Master's* golf tournament." Only one Master down at Augusta? Hardly (and, besides, this famous tournament belongs in the no-apostrophe camp: *Masters*). And a Texas jamboree described in *American Profile* as the Old *Timer's* Reunion actually drew not one but a number of veteran rodeo performers. Much of the time, it's clear, writers are sure they need to insert an apostrophe somewhere, but they really don't know just where it should go. Sometimes, as noted, they're wrong—they need no apostrophe at all.

I myself jotted down the most quietly spectacular example of this point I've ever seen, having pulled off the highway to make the note. A convenience store in a small town bore this sign: ALWAY'S OPEN.

In describing a tour to Dollywood, the Tennessee theme park named for the country star Dolly Parton, the *Lexington Herald-Leader* produced a two-apostrophe sentence, one right, one wrong: "The Great Smoky Mountain's National Park is only a stone's throw away." The "stone's throw" is fine, of course—one stone, thus an apostrophe plus an *s*—but there are many mountains, not just one. In splitting the *s* off from *Mountains*, however, the editors make the word appear to be singular. In accordance with the rule, they should have said *Mountains*, and with no apostrophe at all, because this is not a possessive situation but is merely descriptive. The writer probably became confused because the name of the park has an *s* in it; actually, the name is no more possessive than Yellowstone Park or Bryce Canyon. Even if it were a possessive, however, it would be unlikely to be adorned with an apostrophe; Martha's Vineyard is one of the very few American geographic spots that retain the apostrophe in their names, and in Britain the survivors include Land's End, at the southwestern tip of England, and John o' Groat's, at the northern tip of Scotland.

Moving to hills in the American West, we read in a *New York Times* story on the development of the atomic bomb that "the drama began in earnest when Los Alamos ('the poplars') was founded in 1943 at what had been a rustic *boy's* school in the New Mexico mountains." A school for just one boy? Ah, tragedy! When the scientists turned that lone rustic lad out of his school, what became of him? Whither across the earth did the poor youngster wander?

Recognize, however, that all plurals are not formed by adding *s* to the noun, and use the apostrophe accordingly. Since *children*, for instance, is already plural, to make it possessive add an apostrophe and *s*: *children's*. But note how often you see such forms as *childrens'* and *peoples'* (meaning not the Asian, African, and other peoples of the world but simply the people of a particular place). Quoting Rory Kennedy, a social-activist filmmaker who is the youngest daughter of Ethel and the late Senator Robert F. Kennedy, editors had her saying, "What always makes a difference is a community of social programs and services which are giving attention to these *peoples'* needs," when she was merely saying "the needs *of these people.*"

Some names acquire a possessive quality because the speaker has a false model in mind. Thinking, apparently, that all physical disorders called by proper names acquire these names from the scientists associated with them, people speak, for instance, of *Lyme's* disease, parallel to Bright's disease or Hansen's disease, though the name comes from the place in Connecticut in which the disorder was first identified. (If it were named after the doctor who first recognized what it was, it would be called Steere's disease.)

Since, however, no one supposes that groundhogs had anything to do with the special name given to February 2, the usage *Groundhog's* Day must be attributed to simple carelessness. Thus we can say, with considerable technical accuracy, that you're unlikely to contract *Lyme* disease on *Groundhog* Day (because the ticks that carry the spirochete don't flourish in wintry weather). One way to earn the grouchy grammarian's favor, I assure you, is to get names right; for him, it's both simple and important.

Syntax often poses a problem for the person who is determined to get that apostrophe in somewhere. "Always fond of a constructive nightmare," a writer whose work appears in a *New Yorker* travel advertisement tells us, "I was enthralled when invited this summer to be part of a small American documentary crew travelling to Baghdad with individuals famously despised by powerful persons in both *nation's* governments." Since the writer is talking about the governments of both nations, he needed to use the plural: *nations'*.

Somewhat sadly, my friend declared that many writers use apostrophes in their work with no more logic than if their pet parakeets had flown back and forth across the pages, dropping their tiny loads among the printed words as necessity, or the spirit, moved them.

"Some years ago, Parrish," he told me, "a poor old distraught professor claimed that he had inserted at least 50,000 apostrophes into papers submitted by his students. Another chap, equally distraught, claimed that he had removed 50,000 apostrophes from his students' work. And I believe both stories!"

THE GROUCH'S REMINDERS

- Never split a word apart to insert your apostrophe.

- For most nouns, add *'s* to make a singular possessive, add *s'* to make a plural possessive.

- To form the possessive of a plural noun that doesn't end in *s*, add *'s* as you would with a singular noun: *children's, oxen's.*

- The possessive form of the names of institutions, enterprises, associations, and publications often drops the apostrophe: teachers college, *Publishers Weekly.*

It's a Contraction— Really

One blunder associated with the apostrophe so irritates my grouchy friend that he ordered me (yes, ordered me!) to give it separate treatment. He may not have realized, however, that the first example I would find would come from a fund-raising letter sent out by a nonprofit organization he admires (for, beneath it all, the old grump actually has quite a charitable soul): "[C]ountless Tibetans have died since 1949, when the Chinese government established *it's* presence in the region."

As my friend says, the confusing of *it's* with *its* is enormously, incredibly common. Perhaps people believe that in speaking of something belonging (or pertaining) to something else, they must supply an apostrophe—never stopping to think that we don't say *her's* or *your's* or *their's*. We don't do it, at least, when we're on our good behavior, but note how the *New York Times* described the surprising wonders of a labor leader's apartment. There was not only "rosewood galore," there were "his and *her's* bathrooms and his and *her's* dressing rooms (each with three cedar closets)."

A pure, classic example occurs in this sentence from an AP story: "Romandetti said that the remodeling was overdue for many restaurants and that the timing has more to do with [Denny's] improved financial situation than *it's* image."

Speaking of the "tremendous difficulty" experienced by students in coping with the apostrophe, Paul Sawyer, an English professor at Bradley University, noted a number of years ago that the greatest difficulty came with the word *its*. In addition to *its* and *it's*, he said, his students had invented a new form: *its'*. No doubt this creativity represented a response to the working of the "there has to be an apostrophe in there somewhere" principle, and, in fact, these students were not alone in this invention. In 1988, the grouchy grammarian commented in a note attached to the clipping, a merchandising company informed its customers that it was changing "*its'* remittance address."

In a piece on electronic books, the *New York Times* sidestepped the whole issue in this sentence: "The RCA's screen and a relatively high resolution made up for *it* not rendering typefaces as elegantly as [Microsoft] Reader." *Its* is desirable here, because *not rendering*, which is the equivalent of "failure to render," is a gerund (a present participle used as a noun), and the general principle is that a noun or a pronoun preceding a gerund should be possessive.

The central point is that possessive pronouns survive on their own with no help from punctuation. And writers forget that we use the apostrophe to show where letters have been omitted as well as to indicate possession. *It's*, of course, is simply a short way of saying *it is*. You should note, as well, the difference between *who's* (who is) and *whose* (belonging to who[m]), and between *you're* (you are) and *your* (belonging to you).

TV Guide offered a fine example of the latter confusion: "It's OK to hold a pastel pageant [colorless political convention] if *your* trying to get 52 percent of the vote." Indeed, the magazine seems to have a continuing problem in this particular area. In an interview concerned largely with Pamela Anderson's new (postoperative) breast size ("It is not that big *of* a difference," the actress explains),* the reporter comments: "*You're* series, *V.I.P.*, is a hit with viewers." The presence of such errors suggests that the writer really isn't paying much attention to the task at hand. The grouch, shuddering, sees this heedlessness as a rising trend.

THE GROUCH'S REMINDERS

- *It's* is a contraction of *it is*. *Its* (no apostrophe) is the possessive form of *it*.

- *Its'* is not a word at all (and if it were one, it wouldn't have any meaning). Never use it in your writing.

---

*See Topic 19 for more about *of*.

Whom Cares? {16}

Years ago, the *New Yorker* had among its humorous column fillers a popular running item called The Omnipotent Whom, giving examples of the misuse of this little word. Though I haven't seen this feature in the magazine for a long time, the same kinds of provocative uses of *whom* just keep on appearing.

The AP offers us a variant, with *whomever* for *whom:* "The [panel's] advice came amid a drive to push legislation through the House that would double the current presidential pay for *whomever* succeeds President Clinton in January 2001."

What happens in such cases is simply that the writer or the speaker looks at *for* (or any other preposition in a comparable spot) and presumes that the following noun or pronoun is its object. Actually, however, the whole noun clause—here "whoever succeeds President Clinton in January 2001"—is the object of the preposition, and *whoever* is the subject of the verb in this clause. Failure to identify the clause is the root of the *whom* problem.

Nor can we call it a new problem. Back in 1946 we find *Life* magazine saying in an article about the racist Senator Theodore Bilbo of Mississippi that "his favorite target is the Negro, *whom* he claims is constantly being incited . . ." The editors obviously thought that *whom* is the object of "he claims," which actually is only a parenthetical insertion; *who*—as the form should be—is the subject of "is being incited."

Whom turns up in odd places because it is supposed by some to be a nicer, classier, word than *who*, just as *I* is often thought to outrank *me* (between you and *I*), but the supposition is groundless. These are all just words, which belong in some places at some times and not in others at other times.

Whiches, *Who's*, and *Thats* {17}

Although the grouchy grammarian readily grants that sports reporters often give us the most stylistically interesting parts of the news, he grumbles that they tend to display a detachment from basic rules of grammar and usage.

Several years ago a columnist, looking as always to next year, wrote concerning a well-known basketball coach: "[Rick] Pitino mentioned an incoming freshman, *which* he could not name but is obviously highly regarded Wayne Turner of Chestnut Hill, Mass., as [Kentucky's] point guard next season." The "point" here is extremely simple: a person is NEVER a *which*; only a nonperson can be a *which*—a book or a tree or a crocodile. He or she can be a *who* or a *whom* (as should have been the case here), and a person and a nonperson can each be a *that*, as in Mark Twain's novel *The Man That Corrupted Hadleyburg* or Leonard Wibberley's *The Mouse That Roared*. Note that we can use *that* when the clause it introduces is restrictive; that is, when the sentence won't make much sense without this clause. The fact of roaring sets Wibberley's particular "mouse" apart from all other mice, and is thus a restrictive idea; it limits the meaning to this particular mouse.

From time to time through the years, the reputation of *that* has suffered from the false rumor that it should not be used to refer to persons. A modern example comes from Dear Abby, who in a column on "rules of basic grammar" asks readers not to "use the word 'that' when 'who' is correct. ('That' refers to inanimate objects, 'who' to people.)" Well, not so. It's hard to know where this deprecation of *that* came from, since it has been used in references to people for hundreds of years; as Webster sums it up, "the notion that *that* should not be used to refer to persons is without foundation; such use is entirely standard."

An interesting point here, however, is that when speaking of a specific person or persons, people have traditionally tended to prefer *who*, as in "Wilson was the president *who* ordered troops into Mexico," and have used *that* when the reference is general, as in the Mark Twain and Leonard Wibberley book titles or in "Who was it *that* told you?" or "All the members *that* were present supported the resolution." The best advice comes from Follett and Barzun, who suggest that in restrictive clauses you choose *who* or *that* depending on which one produces "greater ease and naturalness" in the sentence.

Just as a person is not a *which*, a nonperson should not be referred to as a *who*, not even in such spicy and provocative items as this one from the *New York Times*: "Some of the female chinook salmon *who* spawn along a stretch of the Columbia River in Washington State hold a secret: They began life as males." *Who* means what or which person (or persons), but, apparently extending the idea of personhood, the *Times*'s own style manual allows the use of *who* for an animal if its sex is known or if it has a personal name. Even under that principle, however, the status of the epicene chinook remains, at best, murky.

Grammarians and students of style have written thousands of words, many of them contradictory, on the nature and uses of *that* and *which* as relative pronouns. In the grouch's well-thumbed copy of the original edition of *Modern English Usage*, published in 1926, H. W. Fowler observed that if the language had been "neatly constructed by a master builder who could create each part to do the exact work required of it," then *that* and *which* could fill specific roles instead of overlapping, as they do.

Fowler noted the widespread and quite false idea that *which* holds a higher rank than *that*—*which* supposedly being literary and *that* colloquial; this belief sometimes leads writers to change a mental *that* into a written *which*. (In the same way, the grouch remarked in one of our little talks, people seem to regard *I* as higher class than *me*; he sees this as one of the reasons people say things like "*My* aunt gave the property to my brother and *I*.") Far from accepting this class idea, Fowler, in his discussion of *that* and *which* as relative pronouns, made a famous case for giving each word a specific assignment: *that* to be the restrictive relative pronoun and *which* the nonrestrictive. But, he conceded, "it would be idle to pretend that it is the practice either of most or of the best writers."

As the years passed, this point proved to be perfectly right. Note Graham Greene: "[H]is humorous friendly shifty eyes raked her like the headlamps of a second-hand car *which* had been painted and polished to deceive." Note, years later still, Anita Brookner: "Occasionally Mme Doche took pity on him and served him a plate of the thick gruel-like soup *which* she made for her employer's evening meal." Each of the clauses introduced by *which* is "defining," as Fowler called it.

Thus, obviously, Leonard Wibberley would not have been incorrect if he had called his book *The Mouse Which Roared*, but he felt, as does the grouchy grammarian and as do many—nowadays, perhaps most—careful writers that *that* reads better in such instances. But to flatly declare *which* wrong in such cases, as some writers on grammar and usage have done in recent years, is to display arbitrariness far beyond any strictures of the grouchy grammarian. "Anyone who likes to do so may limit his own *that*'s to defining clauses," write Bergen Evans and Cornelia Evans in their classic *Dictionary of Contemporary American Usage*. "But he must not read this distinction into other men's writing."

The distinction must not be read, for instance, into the writing of such diverse and much-admired stylists as Winston Churchill, T. S. Eliot, Elizabeth Hardwick, Dean Acheson, and George F. Kennan, each of whom on occasion employed a restrictive *which*, as FDR likewise did when he called December 7, 1941, "a date *which* will live in infamy."

Punctuation plays a part here, too. What definitively marks a restrictive clause is that it is not set off by commas. It's the difference between "the mouse that roared" and "the mouse, which I knew well, roared"; the latter example presumes that we know which mouse is being talked about and merely gives us some information about it.

(For the record, I must point out that Wayne Turner not only became the Kentucky point guard, as Coach Pitino anticipated, but played important roles on two national championship teams.)

THE GROUCH'S REMINDERS

- A person is a *who* or a *whom*, never a *which*.

- Both a person and a nonperson can be described as *that* (The Man *That* Corrupted Hadleyburg, The Mouse *That* Roared).

- In general, try to use *that* when the clause it introduces is restrictive; that is, when the sentence won't make much sense without this clause.

Where's the Irony?

Many journalists have fallen into the habit of using *ironically* to mean simply *coincidentally*: "Ironically, NFL passing champion Warren Moon . . . suffered the same injury two weeks earlier in a 40–20 loss to the Bengals." Coincidentally, yes, of course. Unfortunately, certainly. But wherein, indeed, lies the irony?

You have irony when you are expressing a meaning opposite to the normal sense of the words. If an associate bungles an assignment and you tell him "Nice work!" that's irony. If he does the same thing again next week, he hasn't performed an ironic action, he has merely displayed incompetence. What you say to him then is up to you.

The Intrusive *Of* ⟨19⟩

Whether it should be blamed on teenagers or it arose from some other group's willfulness, a wholly unnecessary and undesirable *of* keeps popping up in otherwise respectable sentences.

After a competition, for example, an interviewer asked a participant: "Were you surprised at that close *of* a race?"

Discussing the movement of a winter storm, a CNN weather forecaster assured viewers that "the snow shouldn't be that big *of* a factor."

From a recent newspaper interview: "'I'm not that highbrow *of* a person,' Johnson said."

Sometimes, one fears, the reporter has put this usage into the mouth of a literate interviewee who actually didn't employ it, but the poor interviewee has no defense when the newspaper has appeared or the quote has gone out over the air. That could be the case in the next sentence, in which the reporter uses an indirect quote: "Western Kentucky women's basketball coach Paul Sanderford didn't think Tennessee's women would have that big *of* an advantage playing at home."

The first of these examples differs from the other two in an important way. In describing the race as *that close*, the interviewer and the participant had an objective fact as a point of reference: a close race had just taken place. But the sentence should simply say "that close a race," with no *of*.

In the latter examples, however, the writers are employing the currently popular and quite vague *that* without anchoring it to any base or fact. How big is *that big?* They couldn't tell you. They just mean big.

The forecaster needs to say that "the snow shouldn't be a big factor."

Johnson can assure us: "I'm not a particularly highbrow person."

The reporter can let us know that "Sanderford didn't think that Tennessee's women would have a significant advantage."

Of is to be used when a comparison is being made—Johnson is more, or less, *of* a highbrow than Meiners is—or a statement is being made about degree: much *of* or little *of,* most *of* or none *of.*

On the other hand, writers following a regrettable current trend are removing *of* where it is needed or at least is desirable. Describing an evening spent at a magic show, a columnist noted that after disappearing from the stage, the performer reappeared "rising from a platform in the audience a *couple hundred feet* away." That sounds like a replay of rapid-fire Broadway talk from *Guys and Dolls* several generations ago. "Couple *of* hundred," though lacking any grace, would be a great improvement. The general contemporary move toward terse and even curt speech, the grouchy grammarian feels, should not result in pidgin English.

Preposition
Propositions

In a general way, the grouchy grammarian expressed both concern and puzzlement on reading the following sentence and many others like it: "With no regard for health, the show biz industry has *imposed* impossible standards *for* women." What concerned him was the faltering uncertainty that characterizes this assertion. If the industry was imposing standards, it had to impose them *on* somebody. Was it imposing them *on* women, or was it imposing standards *for* women *on* some other group?

Prepositions have been around a long time, my friend notes, but nowadays a great many speakers and writers seem awkwardly self-conscious in their presence. The result is often an unnatural or unidiomatic use of a simple preposition like *on* or *for*, as in the preceding example.

What, exactly, is a preposition? The general definition is broad and vague—a preposition is a word that shows the relation of a noun or a pronoun to another word or element of a sentence—but you might keep it in mind as you look at all the examples in this topic. You might also remember two points Wilson Follett and Jacques Barzun make in their book *Modern American Usage*: (1) One of the greatest difficulties in learning European languages is "the mastering of the idiomatic use of prepositions with verbs, adjectives, and nouns," and English is particularly troublesome; (2) "nothing gives away the foreign speaker or the insensitive writer like the misused preposition." I see this insensitivity as the equivalent of the grouch's "faltering uncertainty."

Particularly striking is a strange paradox concerning the preposition *of*. In Topic 19 we saw how it intrudes where it isn't needed, but now we must look at the increasing use of another preposition, *for*, where normal and established idiomatic English calls for *of*. Weather reporters keep giving us such information as this: "There's a thirty percent chance *for* rain tomorrow," and a CNN forecaster spoke of "the threat *for* showers" (the threat for showers to do what?). Forecasters would do better to say "chance *of* rain" and, certainly, "threat *of* showers." *Of* is value neutral—we may want it to rain or we may not. *For*, on the other hand, implies that we hope it will rain. "There's a chance *for* me to go to Yale," for instance, conveys the thought that the speaker, for whatever reason, wants to go to Yale, perhaps is even dying to go to Yale.

Another context in which we often find *for* used for *of* is illustrated in this description of a Cincinnati business executive, who is identified as "vice president and treasurer *for* Procter & Gamble." The point here is that you are president *of* the United States or secretary *of* a chess club—you're an officer *of* the organization. If you're a vice president *for*, then it's *for* a particular area, such as finance or development (and, indeed, that's really short for vice president *of* the company *for* finance, etc.).

For unfathomable reasons (the insensitivity mentioned in Follett-Barzun?), writers frequently go to great lengths to avoid being associated with *of*. A Knight Ridder obituary article described Rev. Leon Sullivan, the Philadelphia pastor who helped bring down South African apartheid, as "the first black board member at General Motors and a confidant *to* many business leaders." "The first black member of the General

Motors board" might have been a neater way to make that point, but the real issue here is *to* rather than a normal *of* after "confidant."

A similar shunning of *of* appeared in an AP story about the actor Ed Harris, who was chiefly responsible for the making of the movie *Pollock*. We are told that "Harris grew fascinated with [Jackson] Pollock after reading biographies *about* the painter in the mid-1980s." Harris had certainly read *books about* Pollock, but he had read *biographies of* Pollock.

Still a different side-stepping turned up in a small-town newspaper, which, in accordance with our ground rules, shall go unidentified. An article about a forthcoming performance by two violin-playing sisters refers to them as "natives *to* Poland." This description has a botanical or zoological sound, though not as much so as it would if "natives" were singular: "the Bengal tiger is native to Nepal"; "the sisters are native to Poland." The sisters, whose accomplishments show that they are extremely talented and whose photograph shows that they are extremely attractive, are, in fact, natives *of* Poland.

An NPR news program produced its own distinctive example of *of*-avoidance. Discussing the career of the Czech-born symphony conductor Rafael Kubelik, the reporter noted that "in 1948 Kubelik fell afoul *with* the newly installed [Communist] regime in Czechoslovakia." This actually looks as though the reporter had merely reached into a barrel and pulled out the first preposition available, which, regrettably, did not prove to be *of*.

One of the nicest distinctions in English involves the prepositions *to* and *with*; it's efficient and economical, and it's also a distinction that seems in danger of disappearing. Look at this sentence from an AP report on electric-power rationing in Brazil: "Households consuming an average of more than 200 kilowatts per hour each month . . . would have to reduce their consumption by 20 percent compared *to* last year." Then consider the following sentence from the *New York Times* obituary of the sculptor Benjamin Karp: "The art critic Leo Stein, brother of Gertrude Stein, praised Mr. Karp's work and compared his drawings *with* Picasso's." What these sentences need to do is swap prepositions, with *to* replacing *with* before "Picasso's," and *with* moving over to precede "last year."

Why are these changes needed? Reflect on one of the most famous lines in Shakespeare's sonnets: "Shall I compare thee *to* a summer's day?" Compare *to* here means *liken:* Shall I tell you how much you resemble a summer's day? In the sentence from the *Times*, Leo Stein is likening Karp's drawings to Picasso's. On the other hand, compare *with* means to *make a relative assessment*, and thus often to find differences, which is the point in the sentence about electricity in Brazil: Power consumption will be 20 percent less compared *with* [what it was] last year. The grouch would be delighted to see this *to-with* distinction preserved.

In deference to my grumpy friend, I insert here, since it concerns a mild little preposition, a point he urged me to include: One graduates *from* high school, but one does not graduate high school. The school is already divided into levels—grades—before we arrive. When I observed to my friend that some dictionaries record "graduate high school" as an acceptable usage, he responded with the cold stare I had come to know well. Had I heard anyone whose speech and writing I admired use it? No, I had not. That was that. (*Graduate* also means to grant degrees, thus to produce graduates: The college *graduated* 347 yesterday. So, though you can't graduate your high school, your high school can graduate you—provided, of course, that you meet the requirements.)

Finally, I mention a delightful, if unintended, contribution from an anonymous reporter who described an acrimonious discussion as breaking up when one of the participants departed "*with* a huff." With a puff, too, no doubt! And maybe he even blew somebody's house down.

THE GROUCH'S REMINDERS

- A preposition is a word that shows the relation of a noun or a pronoun to another word or element of a sentence.

- Avoid using the preposition *for* when you mean *of:* chance *of* rain, secretary *of* a chess club. You can be a vice president *of* Procter & Gamble, as well as a vice president *for* finance.

- Compare *to* means to liken to. Compare *with* means to make a relative assessment.

But Won't You Miss Me? {21}

As I mentioned earlier, the topics in this book vary from the general to the word specific. This latter group includes some of my grouchy friend's greatest pet peeves (although I don't actually believe he looks on them as pets of any kind). Judging by the frequency with which he mentioned it, it was one of his favorites—in this negative context—that quite movingly turned up one day on the sports page.

During 2001, the Florida basketball coach, Billy Donovan, had to say good-bye to an outstanding player who was declared ineligible because of what the campus police termed "minor gambling infractions." Probably the first truly outstanding player recruited by Donovan, the player had served as a kind of good-luck charm, since a number of other high school stars had followed him to the Gainesville campus. Donovan would certainly feel his absence. But here is what the coach said: "I love Teddy. There are people who do things wrong, but I will stand by him the rest of his life. I think he knows in his heart that I'm behind him. *I'll miss not having him around.*"

That one made the grouch cackle, partly, I know, because one hears it frequently, and partly because it had once or twice been said to him and he didn't much like it. I certainly wouldn't want to tell him *not* that I would miss seeing him, but that I would miss *not* seeing him. And he's absolutely right about the widespread use of this expression. TV actors gaze into each other's eyes and murmur it soulfully, and no one ever seems insulted by it.

But now you, at least, know better.

Well, Better, Best, Most {22}

In an article about the son of Bill Curry, the former Alabama and Kentucky football coach, a reporter calls the young man "the youngest of two Curry children." Is it possible, the grouchy grammarian wondered in a marginal note, that a newspaper writer had never learned that one person is *young*, one person is *younger* than another person, and one person is the *youngest* of three or more? These adjectival levels are called positive, comparative, and superlative. In speaking of Curry's two children, we of course need to use the comparative. If the coach and his wife should have another child, then this welcome newcomer will be the youngest of the three Curry children. (When, yielding to strong temptation, I observed to my grouchy friend that Nathaniel Hawthorne had, at least once, used the superlative for the comparative, and so had Emerson, he barely bothered to give me the familiar stare.)

A different kind of problem can arise with the comparative *more* and the superlative *most*, as in this sentence from the *New York Times:* "[H]er research found that married couples were generally *more* financially *well* off than couples who simply lived together." The word for *more well*, of course, is *better*.

The following sentence from the *New Yorker* needs a touch of the analogous remedy: "Gershon Salomon . . . has become one of the *most well*-known advocates of removing the mosques in order to rebuild the Temple right away"; Salomon, that is, is one of the *best*-known.

The same problem arose in this discussion by an AP baseball writer of a Washington pitcher's (yes, Washington once had a major-league team and may have one again) 1962 feat of striking out twenty-one batters in a sixteen-inning game: "While [Tom] Cheney's total remains the highest in a major league game, it's certainly not one of baseball's *most well-known* marks."

A sentence that received criticism in Topic 2 here shows a redeeming side: "The *best known* of the previous biographies . . . is that by Enid Starkie, who carried out much of the documentary scholarship on which our knowledge of Rimbaud's 'lost years' are based." This sentence from the *Times Literary Supplement* has its obvious subject-verb-agreement problem, but it gives us a good example of the use of *best* instead of *most well* before an adjective.

THE   GROUCH'S   REMINDER

Use the superlative form of an adjective (*best, most, fastest, youngest*) only when three or more items or individuals are being compared. When you're talking about two items, use the comparative (*better, more, faster, younger*).

Between *Who* and *What?* Prepositions with More Than One Object {23}

For some years now, linguistics professors have been telling us that English will ultimately drop one of the two cases in which certain pronouns come. Perhaps so. Meanwhile, however, these scholars continue to pay careful attention to the difference between the nominative and the objective—they wouldn't be caught dead saying "to *she* and *I*"—and, says the grouchy grammarian, so should anybody who claims the title of communicator or reporter or, indeed, anybody else.

Nevertheless, the Associated Press copy chiefs failed at this task in this basketball report from State College, Pennsylvania: "Penn State's Greg Bartram knew there was contact between *he* and Indiana's Chris Reynolds with the game on the line near the end of regulation."

Here we have, in grammatical terms, a compound object of the preposition *between*, and compound objects seem to possess some quality that makes normally reasonable people forget linguistic common sense. A person who would never say anything so unnatural as "she gave the present to *I*" will often—and quite readily—say "she gave the present to *he* and *I*," as if by being a double object an object ceased to be an object at all.

A newspaper column informs us that former President

Jimmy Carter felt that he had faced much unfair criticism, "with *he* and his family often depicted as 'hillbillies.'"

Although not a member of the media, Mark McGwire was widely and memorably quoted during 1998 on his way to his remarkable seventy–home run season.* Hence it may not be too unfair to cite him in the present context. Speaking of his nip-and-tuck race with his friendly rival, Sammy Sosa, McGwire said, "We've been going back and forth. It's been a tremendous ride for *he* and *I*." (At least, that's what the *New York Times* said he said.)

You know now—don't you?—that after *with* or *for* you must have an objective pronoun. The columnist writing about Carter should have said "with *him* and his family . . ." McGwire should have said "for *him* and *me*," or, more likely, "for *us*." After a preposition, a personal pronoun—or a hundred personal pronouns—must appear in the objective case. My friend allows no exceptions.

*A remarkable but not enduring record; it would stand for only two seasons.

Other . . . or *Else*   {24}

good sentence and a well-furnished room have much in common. Each has its large, prominent items—piano and couch, subject and verb—and also a number of smaller items that increase its usefulness and appeal—end tables and paintings, adjectives and subordinate conjunctions. (I realize that I'm shifting here from the grouchy grammarian's view of the sentence as a car engine, but it's merely a temporary departure.) Sometimes words that seem modest and quiet make important contributions to the clarity of a sentence.

Such a word is missing in this verdict on the Iraqi dictator Saddam Hussein delivered by a Cox Newspapers columnist: "Hussein has authored more human misery than any practitioner in the horrid arts today." As written, this sentence does not include Hussein among the practitioners of "horrid arts," but the writer clearly didn't intend to exclude him. What the writer meant was "any *other* practitioner." To date, Hussein has gone right on practicing. (Although the grouchy grammarian readily acknowledges that a great many English verbs have always come from nouns and certainly raises no objection to this fundamental process—indeed, where would English find itself without it?—he declares that he finds *author* as a verb hackleraising. He has no plan, however, to make a public attack on it.)

"[Representative Sidney Yates, D-Ill.] has served longer than anyone in the House." This sentence, from an AP story, seems to tell us that Yates has not only served longer than all his colleagues but has even managed to outlast himself. The writer needed *else* to do the work performed above by the addition of *other* to the sentence about Hussein.

As is often the case, however, this area of discussion can see surprising switches take place. Discussing the family background of Orlando "Tubby" Smith, a leading college basketball coach whose career has seen him serve at Tulsa, Georgia, and Kentucky, a sportscaster, properly impressed with the fact he was about to give us, described the coach as "one of sixteen *other* siblings." Now there's an *other* we don't need! In fact, it's almost surreal.

Lie, Lay {25}

Lie, lay, lain
Lay, laid, laid

There they sit (or, perhaps, recline), a handful of little words—the principal parts of the verbs *lay* and *lie*—that seem to cause writers and speakers a disproportionate amount of trouble. Or, to adapt a thought from *Julius Caesar*, does the problem lie in us, that we are inattentive users? As we're all supposed to have learned during the lower grades, *lie* means to recline and *lay* means to place or put. *Lay* is transitive (takes an object): *Lay* the book on the table. *Lie* does not take an object: When I want to take a nap, I *lie* down. What compounds the problem is the appearance of *lay* in both sets of principal parts; the grouch and I both regret it, but we can't help it.

By far the most common error, which seemed to accelerate in the linguistically as well as politically turbulent 1960s, is the use of *lay* and *laid* for *lie* and *lay*: "Donna Reed discovered it would take more than hard work to secure the bright and promising future that seemed to *lay* ahead," declared the narrator on an A&E network biography.

"[T]he six participants *laid* down on the hogan's earthen floor to sleep around 4 a.m." (AP).

An Indian potter "talks about some of her pottery—small, delicately sculpted face pipes and wedding jugs—*laying* on the kitchen table of her modest home" (*American Profile*).

A mailer from *National Geographic Adventure* gives us some appalling information about the Congo: "A croc hits you with his tail, then drags you to the bottom and *lays* on you until you are drowned. Then he hauls you to the shore and eats you there." (Just exactly what, we must ask, does this croc lay on you?)

My grouchy friend ascribes this *lay*-for-*lie* tendency, in its early stages, to willful heedlessness on the part of younger speakers; it was fun to be incorrect—then, as time went on, he says, ignorance took over.

One eminent baby boomer—a Rhodes scholar, at that—shocked a Florida observer by speaking, in a Memorial Day address, of "America's fallen soldiers *laying* in the field." Well, said the Floridian in a letter to the *Sarasota Herald Tribune*, "of all [Bill Clinton's] peccadilloes, this may be the most reprehensible." After all, the correspondent said, "hens lay eggs; presidents should not."

But something of a backlash also exists. Some writers seem to have become so self-conscious or insecure over the *lie-lay* problem that they have consigned *laid* to the list of bad words and simply refuse to use it even where it's called for. A striking example of this foible comes from an unsuspected (at least by me) part of my friend's archives. A page from what is very obviously a steamy story (in the grouch's files? Good grief!) contains this sentence: "He pulled her down and *lay* her over the windowsill like a seesaw." Another such sentence, from a different sexual angle: "[S]he grasped my lips firmly between hers as she *lay* her hands on me, one on each breast." How did these torrid examples come to my friend's attention? I didn't ask, and he didn't tell.

Much more conventionally, the *New York Times* said in a story looking back to the Soviet blockade of Berlin in 1948: "On June 24 Stalin *lay* siege to the city's three western zones."

This same confusion erupted in horrendous form in a British novel, *Tongues of Flame*, in which a visiting American evangelist, one Joy Kandinsky, approached the worshippers and "*lay* white hands on them all at the front." By the time a British cleric makes a similar move, twenty-five pages farther on, the editors have become so frazzled that they allow (or, possibly, produce) this sentence: "Father put down the daffodils and his hat and *layed* his hands over Rolandson's on Adrian's forehead."

Remember that *lay* is something you do to an object, *lie* is something you do with your own body; *lay* takes an object, *lie* does not. Remember, also, to use the right past-tense form.

Several years ago *A Current Affair* offered an amusing footnote to the *lie-lay* question, when we learned that a certain columnist "*lays* down the gauntlet." Grammatically, that's impeccable, but what a gentle move to make with that ancient symbol of challenge, a knight's glove! Usually, a gauntlet is thrown or flung down, thus setting the tone for the combat to follow. It's an idea my grumpy friend thoroughly understands.

THE GROUCH'S REMINDER

If you're talking about an action that involves an object, say *lay*. Say *lie* when you're describing what you do when you stretch out on a couch. And remember, especially, that the past tenses are tricky, because the past tense of *lie* is *lay*. That's just the way it is. (Your best bet is to memorize the two short lines at the beginning of this topic.)

A Case of
Lead Poisoning {26}

Lead: a heavy, soft, malleable metal, my dictionary tells me. The word is pronounced to rhyme with *bed.* It is, of course, a noun.

Lead: a verb meaning to guide, to direct, and so forth. It is pronounced to rhyme with *seed.* Its past-tense form is *led*—and here is where a great many writers encounter trouble.

This simple example from *TV Guide* illustrates the point: "Parker goes back in time with orders to kill the person who deciphered a CIA code that in turn *lead* to the murder of dozens of field agents." The writer means that the decrypting of the code *led* to the murders.

Now we can introduce a small complication. There's also another *lead,* an adjective describing someone in a foremost or front position, and it finds particularly frequent use with reference to musicians. It is also pronounced to rhyme with *seed.*

Look at this closely packed example, from Time-Life Records, that turned up in the grouch's mailbox. Having enticed the recipient into reading a quiz on pop musicians, it asks: "What very young girl group—the *lead* singer was just 16—*lead* the pack to #1 in Nov. 1964?" "*Lead* singer," the standard term, was just fine there, but after the second dash the writer heard in his or her ear the sound of the past tense, a sound rhyming with *bed*, but unfortunately chose the spelling of the soft, malleable metal. What LEED singer LED the pack? Those are the sounds we want.

Lead is simply not the past form of *lead*; as the grouchy grammarian comments, that's about all you can say. But you may have to say it quite often.

Silly Tautologies {27}

As my friend inelegantly put it one day, "If you have to pay for it, it ain't a gift." He proffered this comment after reading a solicitation in which a magazine publisher offered him a *free gift* in exchange for a subscription.

He also responded badly to a fund-raising letter from a public-service organization, not because he disagreed with the purposes for which the chairman sought support but because of this sentence: "[T]here's one area of the federal budget where *both* political parties *agree*." "Look at this, Parrish," he said with disgust. "It really does take *two* to tango, or to agree—*one* can't do it. Therefore, *both* here is a foolish piece of redundancy. *Both* political parties can *say*, or they can *maintain*, but if you have to make sure that people know you're talking about two and you want to say *agree*, say *the two* parties agree or even go so far as to name them."

You say *both* in a situation in which each of the involved parties can act independently; that is, each one can *believe* or each one can *maintain*, but by definition it takes two (or more, of course) to *agree*. That's why saying *both agree* is redundant—unless both are agreeing with a third party.

The situation is similar in this sentence about a couple that established a bed-and-breakfast establishment in Oregon: "It was the *combination* of *both* house and town that persuaded the Lewises" *(American Profile)*. Neither a *house* nor a *town* can be a combination, which requires the two of them. Hence *both* is superfluous. The same point about *combination* occurs in this discussion of interior decoration: "I like *combinations* of *both* fresh and faux" flowers (Knight Ridder).

A different example of the use of the needless *both* comes from a writer commenting on a long lockout in the National Basketball Association: "*Both* sides are widely separated on how many players would contribute to the escrow fund." This sentence is actually misleading, at least temporarily, because one first looks to see what third party both sides are separated from. But nobody's there, of course—*the two* sides are separated from each other. Parallel to the case with agree, if one side is *separated*, the other is automatically *separated*, too. *Both* is not only needless here, it is inappropriate.

A slightly more challenging instance turns up in a column by William F. Buckley. Speaking of John Adams and Thomas Jefferson, Buckley noted the ever striking fact that "*both* men died on the *same* day, the Fourth of July, 1826." The redundancy here is perhaps a shade subtler than we see in *both . . . agree*, but a simple question will make it clear: Would anyone say that *both* died on *different* days? *Same* is implied in *both;* hence deletion of "the same day," which dilutes the sentence, would give it a keener edge.

One of the in-flight magazines produced what's probably the all-time topper in the *both* department when, in talking about two young brothers, it observed that "*both* were *twins*" (and, of course, it isn't remarkably unusual to hear someone speak of *two twins*).

In the same vein, the grouch snorts at "connected by a *common bond*" and "*sharing the same* point of view."

Many of these sillies, as the grouchy grammarian likes to call them, seem to be the result of the speaker's or the writer's failure to think about what he's saying (*Think!* my friend likes to remind you, me, or anybody else). That was probably the case in the creation of this paragraph from *TV Guide*, which summarizes an episode of the comedy *Frasier* thus: "Frasier and Niles try reviving the career of a has-been *theater thespian.*" Aside from the ironic or comic connotation of *thespian*, this tag is pretty much the equivalent of *gridiron football player* or *body-of-water lifeguard*, because *thespian* means actor and nothing else. (Possibly the writer hoped to convey the idea of stage actor as against performer in movies or TV; if so, it would have been better simply to say that.)

Limited thought or attention probably lay behind this bit of tautology from a Discovery Channel program on various anticipated consequences of the Allied capture, during World War II, of a German submarine: "The captured maps would enable the Allies to *exactly pinpoint* the locations of German U-boats." Do we find *inexact* pinpointing anywhere? No, by definition, we do not.

Streaks of one kind or another form favorite subjects of baseball broadcasters and their comrades in other sports, but in talking about these kinds of individual or team performances, the commentators often forget just what the defining word means. Note, for instance, this observation from the telecast of a Cincinnati Reds game: "Casey's hit stretched his hitting *streak* to ten *straight* games." If it's a *streak*, by definition it's *straight*. The problem this usage highlights is not that the sentence is hard to understand but that inserting *straight* weakens the idea of *streak*, and hence, over a long span of time, one could begin to wonder just what *streak* really means. In other words, this case offers a microcosm of the kinds of habits that cause my grammarian friend much concern.

A similar lack of faith in the meaning of a word is evident in this sentence from the *New Yorker* profile of Jeffrey Archer (see

Topic 1): "At the time he was accused [of involvement with a prostitute], Archer was the deputy chairman of the Conservative Party and a *close confidant* of Prime Minister Margaret Thatcher." Since a *confidant* is a person to whom you entrust your secrets, the two of you are by definition intimates. Adding *close*, like buttressing *streak* with *straight*, actually weakens the statement.

Another word that writers often seem to mistrust is *prerequisite*, which has been established in the language for several hundred years and means something necessary to accomplish a purpose, something you have to have. Like many another writer, however, the author of a book on the famous airship *Graf Zeppelin* displayed limited faith in *prerequisite* by giving it a supposedly strengthening modifier: "Experience, thoroughness, concentration, caution—these are the *essential prerequisites* of the airship commander." And what does *essential* mean? Literally, it describes a quality that is of the essence of a subject, and hence is necessary, something you have to have—just like *prerequisite*. (The words are not full synonyms, but the large area of shared meaning is what concerns us here.) One reason for the popularity of this bit of tautology may be the *pre* before *requisite*, which may mislead some writers into thinking of a prerequisite merely as something that comes first, a preliminary, which may or may not be essential or required.

But, at any rate, the Associated Press sets us straight on the international oil situation. Reporting from Vienna, a correspondent tells us that "OPEC typically acts only with the *unanimous* agreement of *all* its members." Please, sir, we may wonder, just what does *unanimous* mean if it doesn't mean *all*? (On this one, I can truly hear a "Think!" rumbling down the hall.)

A General Electric advertisement in a 1937 issue of a once-influential magazine, the *Literary Digest* (which lost its influence and, soon, its very existence after having predicted that Governor Alfred M. Landon of Kansas would defeat President Franklin D. Roosevelt in the 1936 presidential election), offers a common if not particularly silly example of tautology: "More than forty years ago, [GE scientists] *initiated* the *first* use of electricity in the textile industry." Once you have said *initiated*, of course, you have said *first*. A widely popular variant on this bit of usage is found in statements like this: "When we *first began* dating, we really didn't know each other at all." We commit these little redundancies when we forget that *began, initiated,* and such words have specific meanings related to time and are not simply words of general action: when we *first went out on dates,* or, simply, when we *began dating;* the scientists *initiated the use . . .*

Describing an Eric Rohmer movie, the *New Yorker* commented that "it's all low-key conversation, and there's a *thin veneer* of chic over everybody." Well, says the grouchy grammarian, if you find a *thick* veneer anywhere, cut off a piece of it, wrap it in heavy paper, and send it to him. He promises to refund shipping costs.

THE GROUCH'S REMINDER

Know the meaning of your words, so that you won't weaken your writing and speaking with unneeded or repetitive phrases.

False Series {28}

Here's another look at the earlier *New York Times* sentence from the report of the Georgia Tech–Cincinnati basketball game: "The Yellowjackets also had 27 assists, hit 80 percent of its [*sic*] free throws, and all five starters each scored in double figures." This time we're concerned not with the singular-plural *its-their* scramble but with a structural problem.

"The Yellowjackets also

had 27 assists

hit 80 percent of its free throws . . ."

and then what? If we're going to keep Yellowjackets as the subject, we need a third verb to maintain the parallel structure—perhaps "and *put* all five starters in double figures." As it stands, the series loses its subject, with *starters* replacing *Yellowjackets*. A better solution, as you've probably seen, is to scrap the three-item series by placing *and* between *assists* and *hit* and otherwise leaving the structure unchanged: "The Yellowjackets also had 27 assists and hit 80 percent of [their] free throws, and all five starters each scored in double figures." Of course, the sentence as originally printed had nothing truly puzzling about it, but, as the grouch likes to (and frequently does) say, if you're seeking excellence you will be aware of such points, and if mediocrity satisfies you, you will pay them little heed.

Let's take another example from the world of sports. Speaking of a pro football player who had a troubled career before experiencing a kind of rebirth, an AP reporter noted: "He had been run out of Carolina and New Orleans and accused of being a racist, a quitter and having a drinking problem." The writer could well have said "accused of being a racist and a quitter and of having a drinking problem" or simply "accused of being a racist, a quitter and an alcoholic."

Moving into the bloody realm of conflict in Northern Ireland, we find that on one particular day the police apparently prepared themselves for unusually violent confrontations, as described in an AP story: "The day's tensions began in Ardoyne, a mostly Catholic district, where police *wielding* clubs, shields and *attack dogs*, drove back Protestants who were trying to block a road outside a Catholic elementary school." Police wielding attack dogs? Not really, to be sure; they were wielding clubs and shields and *using* or *employing* attack dogs.

Once you have become aware of the working of a series—A, B, and C are all equal and all have the same form—then you can easily see how to repair faulty ones, like the examples just given.

French Misses {29}

At one time or another, the temptation to jazz up one's prose by inserting a foreign word or phrase proves irresistible to almost everybody who writes. The grouchy grammarian expresses no objection to this practice. Indeed, he says, such expressions often bring something of real value to a sentence; they enhance clarity by expressing an idea for which no true English equivalent exists, they lend an element of grace, or they enrich the sentence by association with the other language: writing well is certainly not unfailingly a matter of buying American.

But when you use a foreign term or phrase, says my crabby friend, you must be "damned sure" you've got it right. If you haven't, you risk turning your reader's or listener's attention away from your subject and onto your inability to discuss it properly. The language that most invites borrowing—and thereby provides the bulk of the troublesome expressions—is, by a wide margin, French. As the grouch said, nobody who's inclined to use *Weltschmerz* has much trouble with it, and as for Spanish, "No way, José" and "el cheapo" and *cojones* are considered sophisticated enough in most circles.

But French . . .

Searching, no doubt, for a well-deserved touch of class, the proprietors of an upscale (as the expression goes) restaurant in

Baltimore advertise a "3 course *pre-fixe* dinner menu." Now, it would certainly be reassuring to know that if you go to this restaurant, your hosts will have decided in advance what they will serve—they will, so to speak, have prefixed the dinner—but in this case one suspects that they intended to say *prix fixe*—a complete meal at a *fixed price*.

An absolutely astonishing example of error came from one of the most fastidious characters in current drama—Niles, of the comedy *Frasier.* In a scene set in a furniture store, this finicky student of wines, paintings, opera, and language itself spoke of a certain item as a *chaise lounge!* Granted, *longue* and *lounge* look a good bit alike, but the Nileses of this world—and their writers and directors—are supposed to know the difference, as should all broadcasters and journalists. A *chaise longue* is simply a *long chair,* and, even though you may sprawl on it in any way you choose, it is only coincidentally a *lounge.* The term *chaise lounge* is also widely used in circles far less lofty than those in which Niles moves; *American Profile*, for example, advises outdoor types that "compact camp stools are better than *chaise lounges.*"

Discussing the adventures in New Hampshire of the two Presidents Bush when each was a candidate—in 1992 George H. W. finished only 10 points ahead of Pat Buchanan, and in 2000 George W. lost to John McCain by 20 points—a *New York Times* columnist commented that "for Bush *fil*, as for Bush *père*, when it comes to the oft-determinative primaries of New Hampshire, there be dragons up there in the hills and notches." Bush *père*— father Bush—is fine. But Bush *fil*—well, *fil* means a number of things, including "edge of the blade," but it doesn't mean "son." That word for that is *fils*. In short, you can't be too careful.

The greatest of all French misses appeared originally in the *Richmond Times-Dispatch* and then as a filler in the *New Yorker* and was saved for posterity by Anne Fadiman in her book *Ex Libris*: "Meanwhile, Richard Parker Bowles, brother of Camilla's ex-husband, Andrew, said that from the beginning Camilla approved of Charles' marrying Diana while she remained his *power mower*." "I have nothing to add to this one!" noted the grouch.

Almost literally tugging at my sleeve, my friend insisted that I not miss the chance here to tell broadcasters and everybody else that if they insist on using the expression *pièce de résistance* on the air or simply in ordinary conversation, they must be aware that, as a French word, *pièce* is not pronounced to rhyme with *grease*. How then? He produced a sort of quiet cackle. "Let them look it up." Uncharitable as that thought may sound, I pass it along as a good motto for anyone adding *vinaigrette* to a list of menu offerings, trying to rent a *pied à terre*, or otherwise using a French expression, naturalized or not, to decorate written or spoken English.

THE GROUCH'S REMINDER

If you want to use a French phrase from time to time, that's fine—but keep a French dictionary handy.

None *Is*, None *Are?*

The grouchy grammarian readily admits to having his own ideas about many points of grammar and usage, but he nevertheless deplores "hypercorrectness," as he somewhat clumsily calls the attempts we frequently see to make rules where none are needed—or should that be "where none *is* needed"?

Is, indeed, *none* singular or is it plural?

As we were talking about this point in general, my friend handed me a comic strip a friend had clipped and sent to him. Unusual—and hence commendable—in having grammar and usage as the subject, the strip, called "Rose Is a Rose," presents us with a woman wearing a whistle, which, she explains to her husband, she intends to blow whenever she witnesses a grammatical error.

"Thank goodness," the husband replies, "none *have* occurred so far today."

The next sound is *FTWEEE*, a blast so loud that it blows the husband off his feet and through a fortunately open window.

Apparently the creator of the strip shares the widespread view that *none* must take a singular verb. It looks like "no one," of course, and it comes from Old English and Old Norse words meaning "not one." But in contemporary English does it mean only *not one* or does it mean, as well, *no persons or things?* The *Oxford English Dictionary* answers the question quite clearly: *none* is most widely used as a plural, and has been so used for many years. The Evanses' *Dictionary of Contemporary American Usage* takes note of an analysis showing that from the time of Sir Thomas Malory to that of John Milton (1450–1650) *none* was treated as a plural once for every three times it was treated as a singular, but then the trend changed; from Milton's era to 1917, *none* was treated as a plural seven times for every four times it was treated as a singular. So it has formidable credentials as a plural, and the trend has increased through the years since that analysis was made.

Some situations, however, obviously call for a singular verb: None of us *is* entitled to be paid before anybody else.

Others just as plainly need the plural: None of the president's advisers *agree* on the significance of the ultimatum.

And one case unmistakably belongs in the singular camp— when *none* means *no part:* None of the mess *has* been cleaned up.

Drug Is a Drag. It Must Have *Snuck* In {31}

Sometimes joke words arise in language and enjoy a good run but then refuse to fade away as they're supposed to do. Unlike the French, the English-speaking world has no language police formally empowered to eradicate bootleg word forms. Even the grouchy grammarian regards this lack as a good thing for English, enabling it to stay fresh and expressive, but it is nevertheless true that as the joke words linger, they fool many people—even some professional users of words—into believing that they're proper words suitable for even serious contexts, and they often achieve wide use.

Reporting a governor's reflections on the duty of citizens to report evidence of criminal wrongdoing, a thoughtful political columnist quoted the governor as saying that it is necessary to be careful in such situations "if you have assets or a reputation that you don't want to have *drug* into court."

A football broadcaster described how many yards a powerful runner *drug* a defensive back. The columnist or the governor or both, together with the sportscaster, obviously believed that *drug* is the standard past-tense form of *drag*, even though no one would follow *tag* with *tug* or *lag* with *lug*. Like these others, *drag* is a simple regular verb; its past-tense form is *dragged*.

Even more widely used is *snuck* as a past-tense form of *sneak*.

It is just as wrong as *drug*. The past tense of *sneak* is *sneaked*. The spiritual leader of this group of words is, no doubt, *brung*, as in "Dance with him what brung you."

Since *drug* and *snuck* are old dialectal forms, you can still run across people here and there, in scattered pockets of the English-speaking world, who employ them quite naturally. These users are entirely different from those who, once upon a time, started saying *drug* and *snuck* just for fun, and you don't find many governors and sports commentators among them. In a note included with this bundle of clippings, the grouchy grammarian expressed his approval of the point made by the *Oxford American Dictionary:* "The past form *snuck* is acceptable only when the writer is attempting to portray regional dialects." As for *drug*, the same dictionary says with admirable terseness: "*Dragged* is the correct past form of *drag*. *Drug* is not."

A related but different blunder came from the Disney studios: *Honey, I Shrunk the Kids.* Didn't at least one person associated with this movie know that *shrank*, not *shrunk*, is the past tense of *shrink*? Or was it that nobody cared? But what was the point of substituting one verb form, though perfectly respectable in its own right and place, for another? At this point, says my old friend, nothing surprises him. He certainly does not give Disney credit for knowing (or caring one way or another) that two or three centuries ago, *shrunk* was common as the past form of *shrink*. If he did give such credit, it would be strictly limited.

Sometimes word forms seems to have been created just to trip us up; even the grouch will make that concession. It would be quite a challenge, for instance, to count all the young (and not so young) sportswriters who have made this mistake: "There were a few boos when Sanders came to the plate in the first inning and *flew* out." What did Sanders do after he landed from his flight? Lay an egg? No, all Sanders had done was hit a *fly* ball, which was caught; therefore he *flied* out.

(This special past-tense form *flied* appears in one other context besides baseball. In the world of the theater, scenery is *flied* when it is raised from the stage into the *flies*, the storage space above.)

THE GROUCH'S REMINDER

Don't confuse informal or joke words with standard forms.

And/Or {32}

When you say *and*, you're adding items together, as in "chocolate *and* pistachio are my favorite flavors." When you say *or*, however, the addition disappears; *or* is what grammarians call a disjunctive—a divider—and when you use it, you're taking the named items one at a time, pointing to one or the other but not to both.

A reporter failed to show awareness of this principle when he wrote: "Several national reports show that people have been injured when bleach *or* ammonia *have* been used as ammunition [for water guns]." If a singular noun follows *or*, then the verb must be singular. But if that following noun is plural, the verb is, of course, plural, too: "Either the Egyptians or the Pakistanis *are* going to supply aid."

When you say *either*, you're also picking one out of two. In looking into high-end Manhattan dining in what he called "depressed times," a *New York Times* reporter asked a lawyer and a consultant flirting at a bar: *Were* either of them cutting back in any way? *Was* is what's needed here.

The same principle applies to *neither* and *nor*. Thus a TV reporter misspoke when, referring to two suspects in a bombing, he said, "Neither *are* being identified as of yet." (See also Topic 10, As of Yet.)

Discussing a much debated air strike in Iraq, a White House official said, "Neither the president nor Dr. [Condoleezza] Rice *were* upset about how the strike was handled."

After talking with Fred Claire, then executive vice president of the Los Angeles Dodgers, about a possible trade, an Associated Press sportswriter told us that "neither Nomo nor Hollandsworth *were* mentioned in his latest talk with Seattle."

In each of these cases, the verb should be singular—*is* and *was*—because *neither* and *nor*, like *either* and *or*, tell us that subjects are being taken one at a time. Failure to recognize this simple fact occurs so frequently that the grouch in one of his bad moments even accused the AP of trying to repeal the meaning of *neither . . . nor*.

Overworked and Undereffective {33}

Happy is the phrase or even single word during the brief time of freshness it enjoys nowadays before overexposure and endless repetition exhaust it. That's the most cheerful observation to be made about: "*Maybe, just maybe*, this Bill-overkill was a declaration of independence." It's probably not fair to single out the columnist Ellen Goodman, who wrote this particular sentence about the attention paid 24/7 by the media to Bill Clinton's well-known problems, since *maybe, just maybe* has become inescapably pandemic. Perhaps, just perhaps, it will disappear like a virus that has infected everybody and thus has done its appointed work.

Let's turn this Topic 33 into a game: See what expressions you can contribute to the cause. You might start with *on the cutting edge* (can you believe that we once lived in a time when nobody spoke of anyone's or anything's being on the cutting edge?) and go on from there.

The grouchy grammarian immediately came forth with *prestigious*, as he recalled an occasion on which the host introduced a visiting speaker as a winner of the "prestigious Pulitzer Prize for history." He considers *prestigious* a perfect example of a useless word, he said. If a prize or a person already possesses prestige, you cannot gild this lily by calling it prestigious (a person who had never heard of the Pulitzer Prize would hardly be swayed by such an adjective); nor, if your subject lacks prestige, can you confer any measure of this quality by applying the word to it.

He accepted my suggestion of *arguably* (Calvin Coolidge was *arguably* America's greatest president; i.e., one can make the case that this was so) as another tired one-word cliché, and I seconded his nomination of *outcomes*, a particularly popular term (for *results*) in education. We agreed that another term, *empowerment*, much used in social contexts with reference to minority groups, faces the danger of losing its edge, and that another social-psychological term, *self-esteem*, similarly suffers from indiscriminate overwork ("Coach told me I got to improve my *self-esteem*"). *Closure* ("the trial and conviction of the murderer gave *closure* to the victim's family") exists in the same state.

It turned out that we both had often laughed (in our differing tones) at the idea of Congressional *oversight*, a term that's not only incessantly used nowadays but that remains as ambiguous as ever. Do we mean *supervision* or do we mean *neglect?*

The grouch and I went on to list expressions that, in complex situations, often substitute for actual analysis: *blaming the victim* and *shooting the messenger,* and *shooting yourself in the foot.* And, to be sure, all fair-minded people favor *a level playing field.*

One-stop shop, a serviceable phrase just a few years ago, is losing its edge, and even the more recent and most efficient *24/7* is itself showing signs of wear and tear.

And now for yours . . .

THE GROUCH'S REMINDER

Don't let a currently popular expression take the place of your own original thought.

Quantities, Numbers {34}

"**M**uch of the added costs [of the space station] *are* due to 18 months of delays." What's wrong here? *Much* refers to an amount of something, and it means a large quantity of it. Because an amount is a mass, a singular entity, *much* as a noun needs a singular verb. What the writer most likely had in mind was *many*, which means not a large mass but a large number of individual items or entities: "*Many* of the added *costs . . . are* due to 18 months of delay." Or he could equally well have said: "*Much* of the added *cost . . . is* due," keeping all the references singular.

A similar problem occurs in the following sentence: "Each year, nearly 75 women apply to the program, but *less* than half are accepted." If these women constituted a mass of woman, then the writer could talk about less than half of it, if he wished. But women are, beyond question, individuals; the writer must therefore speak of number instead of quantity and turn to *few* or *fewer*, in speaking of a small number of them. (For a large number, of course, one would say *many* women and not *much* women.)

Discussion of the weather introduces a special point about expressing quantities. The experts measure rain and snow in inches, but discussion can become a bit tricky because this precipitation falls to the ground in amounts, not in individual inch-sized packets. In describing the effect of a winter storm in the Northeast, the *New York Times* noted that "just over two feet of snow *were* measured in the highlands of northern New Jersey and in the Catskill Mountains." In this context, two feet is a quantity, not an enumeration, and *was* is hence the verb to use here (just as we would say, for example, three months *was* a long time to wait for an answer to a proposal of marriage).

Watering What You're Writing: {35}
The *Alleged* Criminal and the *Alleged* Crime

ost readers of this book are probably not professional journalists or broadcasters, and hence you aren't likely to spend much time writing accounts of crimes and reporting on other police matters. But take a moment, anyway, to notice what the fear of lawsuits has done to the persons who do report on the doings of criminals and supposed criminals. The following description of a drug arrest offers a good lesson in the grouch's favorite recurring theme: THINK about what you're saying.

"According to police reports, Alexander *allegedly* started to run toward the creek, but [Officer] Slone ordered him to stop. Slone ordered the suspect to place his hands on his head, but Alexander *allegedly* tossed something forward into the creek before complying."

Allege, which originally meant to declare under oath, now has the general meaning of asserting without adequate proof; it is a negative word, "colored," as the lexicographer Wilson Follett once noted, "with accusation and criminality."

The second sentence about Alexander and Officer Slone presents no technical problem, although, as is usually the case in such stories nowadays, *allegedly* is heavily overworked; it appears in the same article on two other occasions. But the first sentence is pure gibberish. The reporter did not need *allegedly* or any other such word, because he is not purporting to state incontrovertible fact; the rest of his sentence tells us that the police reports *said* that Alexander started toward the creek. *According to police reports* serves the same function here as *alleged*.

But the reporter didn't dare trust that phrase to do its work. He and his bosses thus allow their apparent continuing trembling fear of lawyers to dictate the watering-down of the prose that appears in their newspaper. Everybody writing for publication should know, however, that, as Bergen Evans and Cornelia Evans note in the *Dictionary of Contemporary American Usage*, inserting *alleged* before an accusation does not automatically confer immunity from prosecution for libel. In fact, libel is such a complex subject that the Associated Press stylebook includes a twenty-page manual on it for the general guidance of writers. (The grouch and I do not purport to give legal advice, of course; we talk about such matters from the point of view of style and effectiveness.)

In view of the accusatory nature of *allege*, the grouchy grammarian felt that a CNN broadcaster was being particularly unfair one day in speaking of the people robbed, raped, and murdered by a serial killer as "*alleged* victims." What had happened to them, after all, was unmistakable; besides, an allegation is a statement about an action, not about the nature of a person. An alleged murder may be one thing, the grouch grumbled; an alleged victim is surely something quite different.*

THE GROUCH'S REMINDER

If you want to water something, make it your flowers rather than your sentences and paragraphs.

---

*For more thoughts on vagueness in language, see Topic 40, Fuzz.

Only But Not Lonely {36}

I n his novel *Howards End*, written early in the twentieth century, E. M. Forster gave the human race a behavioral prescription that has been widely quoted ever since: "*Only* connect." The popularity of this admonition, stressing the prime importance of communication between people, very likely served as one of the important if subtle forces behind the rise, much later in the century, of such phenomena as encounter groups and other interpersonal activities.

Though Forster no doubt offered excellent advice, we're concerned here more with the arrangement of the words than with higher points. You will note that Forster chose not to phrase his admonition as "Connect *only!*" That would be more like a military command than a piece of humanistic counsel, and, as is easy to see, would not have conveyed the feeling the author sought. Besides, his audience might believe that he was telling them to connect but to do nothing else.

But some points about *only* are not so obvious. With respect to its placement in the sentence, *only* has an unusual history; it is, as Sir Ernest Gowers said in *The Complete Plain Words*, a "capricious" word. Since English makes little use of word endings (inflections) to show the role of words in the sentence, this job is performed primarily by sentence order. Normally a modifier comes immediately before the word it modifies: "My grand-mother *hastily* checked the figures." This sentence demonstrates one of the most common sentence patterns: subject, adverb modifying the verb, verb, and object. So common has this arrangement been through the years that it tends to be followed even if the adverb does not modify the verb but relates to another word.

For decades and even centuries, this trend has bothered many commentators on usage, but when I asked the grouchy grammarian about it, he seemed quite unperturbed. "Let's look at *only*," he said. "Of course it ought to stand next to the word it modifies—generally, that is. Certainly you should say 'the facts are known *only* to him' rather than 'the facts are *only* known to him.' And in one particular article the *London Review of Books* would have been well advised to say, 'The Soviet flag flew *only* on official buildings' instead of 'the Soviet flag *only* flew on official buildings,' as if it had some other purpose besides flying but just couldn't manage it."

Then, giving me a bit of a surprise, he said, "Consider the different implications if Patti LaBelle had not called her album 'If *Only* You Knew' but instead had named it 'If You *Only* Knew.'

"But take a sentence like this one: 'After such a misfortune, my luck can *only* get better.' That's English, true English, Parrish. Who in the world would say 'My luck can get *only* better'?

"So *only* is where I part company with the so-called purists, if we still have any of them. This is where people err by being pedantic, not really poorly informed or careless. You know the purists—the people Fowler described as 'clapping a strait waist-coat upon their mother tongue.' Idiom, you know—the characteristic way of saying things—that's important, too.

"A chap named John Bremner made the point perfectly, in his book on words; I have the note here somewhere. . . . Anyway, he said that songwriters need freedom. Who, he wanted to know, would ever call a tune 'I Have Eyes *Only* for You'?

"But I should make one other point. When you're speaking, the emphasis you put on the word helps your listener know immediately what it's doing in the sentence. When you're writing, you need to take greater care."

Pairs—Some Trickier Than Others {37}

Replying to "Sneak-a-Peek Neighbor," an early riser who had the habit of borrowing the morning newspaper from the porch next door before his neighbors got up, Dear Abby said sternly: "The paper belongs to your neighbors. Since they pay for the subscription, they have a right to receive it fresh off the press, not after it's been *rifled* through."

There may be some little idea of thieving here (even though Sneak-a-Peek always returned the paper, and neatly folded, too), but that isn't true in this description of a business executive: "He wants to be able to *rifle* through mail . . . and 'round file' the piles of junk mail that come across his desk" (Knight Ridder).

Both writers mean *riffle* here. Though it shares with *rifle* the idea of going through something, it is a far gentler word, coming from *ruffle* and meaning simply to leaf through; *rifle* is associated with ransacking and looting: The gang *rifled* the apartment. And *rifle* does not need an accompanying *through*. In fact, we can establish a simple rule: if *riffle*, then *through*; if *rifle*, no *through*.

A *New Yorker* writer clearly meant *riffling* in her description of the mother of the then-president of Peru Alberto Fujimori "*rifling* through her daughter-in-law's things." The old lady wasn't looting and plundering, but she was definitely checking up on her son's wife.

Another pair of the kind to look out for: "To whet your appetite for Will Smith's shoot-'em-up western *Wild, Wild West*," notes a Hollywood reporter, "TBS' *Dinner & a Movie* chef wrangled a recipe just for *USA Weekend*." By association with *wrangler* (cowboy), *wrangle* gives the sentence a nice Western flavor, all right, but *wangle* would have been the better choice. To *wangle* is to get your way by cleverness or manipulation, whereas to *wrangle* is to engage in angry argument (and, on occasion, it's true, to get your way by this tactic). Sometimes the underlying thought may simply be that after *wangling* for so long a time, one turns into a *wrangler*.

Despite their similarity, you wouldn't ordinarily think of *buff* and *bluff* as words likely to suffer confusion (certainly no manicurist would think of *bluffing* the nails of the customers), but in recent years the old children's game called blind man's *buff* has acquired a second name: blind man's *bluff*, which, indeed, appears as the title of a book on submarine espionage during the Cold War. In the original name *buff* refers to the three "buffs," or pats (as in buffeting), the blind man earns by catching a player and has nothing to do with bluffing, or fooling, the blind man or anybody else. The move from *buff* to *bluff* offers a good example of the process that students of linguistics call folk etymology, in which a word is replaced by a more familiar word that sounds more or less like it, even if the meaning is quite different.

This next example really isn't especially tricky, but it was said anyway and certainly should be avoided: "I think slot machines are . . . the most *ingenuous* invention ever created or conceptualized . . ." (*N'Digo* [Chicago]). Naive slot machines? A charming idea in this era of the wildfire growth of gambling, but not a charming usage; *ingenious* is required here.

Lose and *loose* wouldn't seem to present much trickiness either; nevertheless, a promotional flier for the Baltimore Symphony admonished patrons: "Hurry! Don't *loose* your seats!" At that, the leaflet perhaps made a point: If you turn your seats *loose*, you certainly *lose* them.

Noting that a reporter had said, with reference to a controversy over the National Rifle Association: "*60 Minutes* has *invoked* the wrath of Charlton Heston," the grouchy grammarian had scrawled along the margin, "I don't think so!" I must agree with that; I cannot believe that CBS would try to employ the wrath of Moses for any conceivable secular purpose. The reporter meant not *invoke* (to call for divine or high human support or protection) but *evoke* (to produce a response).

A similar scramble occurred in a TV movie when a Las Vegas preacher grandly concluded a wedding service by declaring: "By the power *invested* in me by the state of Nevada, I now pronounce you man and wife." The word he needed was simply *vested*—endowed with authority—rather than *invested*, which means what you think it means.

Confusion of *affect* and *effect:* The usual problem here is the use of *effect* where the speaker means *affect:* "The new evening hours don't *effect* me at all." Here the speaker needed to say *affect*, which means to influence or cause a change in its object; to *effect* means to bring about or produce. (The new hours didn't produce the speaker, and they didn't even change his life.) Although *effect* is both a verb and a noun, it usually appears as a noun, as in the expression "the law of cause and *effect*." Correspondingly, *affect* is both a noun and a verb, but we almost always see it as a verb: "The new evening hours don't *affect* me." (As a noun, *affect* is used only by psychologists, both professional and parlor. It denotes a person's style of feeling or emotion.)

Though mention of *complement* and *compliment* appeared in Topic 7, these frequently confused words deserve an encore, partly because of this luxuriant sentence from a food column (*American Profile):* "The sweetness of the melon is enhanced by the black pepper and vinegar and is nicely *complimented* by the smoky flavor of prosciutto."

And these sentences from an interesting AP story also deserve notice: "It is important to point out that men often have a very different perception of sexual harassment. One study from the University of Arizona found that 67 percent of men would feel *complemented* if propositioned by a woman at work, as opposed to 17 percent of women." However inadvertently, one must say, the writer has made a point worth pondering.

Describing a university's efforts to remove a retired professor from his home in order to take over the property as part of the site for a new library, a reporter observed that, as a state agency, the school had the right of *imminent* domain. This is funnier than it probably seemed to the professor, since his protests showed that he saw the university as a juggernaut about to crush him—his destruction was *imminent*. Nevertheless, the word needed here with domain is *eminent*—outranking all other claims and considerations.

An AP sportswriter contributed this example of a frequent confusion: "Arizona's slumping offense provided [Randy] Johnson with another *tortuous* defeat Wednesday night." Since Johnson struck out seventeen batters but still lost the game, he no doubt felt as if he had been tortured, and thus suffered a *torturous* defeat. *Tortuous*, on the other hand, means full of twists and turns—a state of affairs that, unfortunately for Johnson, did not exist in the game in question; his team made only one hit.

Reporting on the rise of a young tennis star, another AP writer declared that "Alexandra Stevenson plays tennis with . . . plenty of *flare*." *Flare* has a number of meanings, all of them relating to the idea of surging or spreading (the *flare* lit up the sky; a wide *flare* marked the once-popular bell-bottoms). What the writer wanted here was *flair*, a talent or special quality; this word has an interesting association, since it means sense of smell in French and hence is associated with the idea of detection. When Sherlock Holmes crawled about on the floor sniffing the scene of a murder, he thus literally displayed his remarkable flair for solving crimes.

Rare, if not unique, is the unintentional scrambling of a proper name and a common noun, but a number of years ago the historian Forrest Pogue, the official biographer of General George C. *Marshall*, observed that the frequent appearance of his subject's name in the press was leading to the corruption of the spelling of the noun (and verb) *marshal*. And so it has proved to be, as a headline in the *Boston Globe* demonstrates. Speaking of a new groundskeeper at the local ballpark, the paper termed him "Fenway's field *marshall*." Likewise, a *New Yorker* book reviewer praised an author who "*marshalls* her arguments with clarity and persuasive force." One more: In discussing World War II in Britain, a brochure promoting *Archaeology* magazine describes a project "to recall the efforts to *marshall* the people in anticipation of a Nazi invasion in 1940." It may be that one will soon have to admit that *marshall* has become the standard spelling.

As verbs, both *avenge* and *revenge* mean the inflicting of injury in return for injury. The noun that goes with *avenge* is *vengeance* ("Vengeance is mine!"), the original concept being that vengeance is retribution for a wrong done to a third party. (When the murdered Julius Caesar fell at the foot of the statue of Pompey, according to a very old work of history, the eyes of the statue looked down on the dead man "and Pompey was avenged.")

Revenge, on the other hand, has always meant paying back someone who has wronged you. Nowadays the verbs *avenge* and *revenge* have become pretty well blended in meaning, so that *avenge* is commonly used regardless of who suffered the wrong (and the sufferer is most likely to be the avenger, since settling matters on behalf of another is not as common in our time as it was in earlier tribal or rural societies). *Revenge* is perhaps more common as a noun: we *seek* revenge more than we *revenge*.

Prominent in the related-but-different category are such pairs as *crumble* and *crumple* and *historic* and *historical*. *Crumple*, indeed, seems to have fallen out of fashion after a long and useful history, even though the meanings are different (folding up but remaining intact as opposed to disintegrating or dissolving). When you read a description of an injured person *crumbling* to the floor, you will know that the writer has borrowed the meaning of *crumple*.

As for *historic* and *historical*, the easiest way to remember the difference is to note that a *historic* event is one that would be discussed at a meeting of a *historical* society.

A promotional mailer for *National Geographic Adventure* quotes an article that appears in the *premier* issue. Although *premier* and *premiere* are indeed forms of the same word, the latter is the one normally used to identify a first performance, appearance, and the like. *Premier*, on the other hand, is another word for prime minister (i.e., *first* minister) and as an adjective means first in rank or precedence.

Like *capital* and *capitol*, these different spellings serve practical purposes. *Premiere* should been the form used in this description (in the *New York Times*) of an unfortunate incident at the Metropolitan Opera, when the British director Graham Vick "came on stage to take a bow at the conclusion of the *premier* of his new production of Verdi's 'Trovatore' and was roundly booed." (It's also true that if the production was receiving its *premiere*, it was ipso facto *new*.)

The narrator on an A&E *Biography* program about the late actor Bob Crane slipped on a very common banana peel when he told us that "*flaunting* tradition, Crane was married on the set of *Hogan's Heroes*." Since there was, in fact, no tradition calling for people in California to come to the set of that TV program in order to get married, the narrator meant *flouting*—disobeying openly and disdainfully—and not *flaunting*—displaying proudly and ostentatiously.

Home as a verb means to proceed toward an objective or a target, and it's the word the writer needed to use in an AP medical story that told us how "long-frustrated researchers are *honing* in on new clues to pre-eclampsia's underlying causes." *Hone* means to sharpen, and without an *on* it sounds even stranger when used to mean *home:* "Guided by media analyst Douglas Rushkoff, ["The Merchants of Cool"] *hones* in the role market researchers, entertainers and a few key corporations play in affecting adolescent choices and behavior." I therefore close this topic with a sharp injunction from the grouchy and apparently long-suffering grammarian: If you're thinking of saying *hone* for *home*, with or without an *on* following the *in*, don't! And, of course, keep your eyes and ears open for all the tricky pairs that swirl around you, in print and sound.

THE GROUCH'S REMINDER

Even words that are closely related can have quite different meanings. Choose the one you really want.

Between vs. *Among* {38}

Many myths persist about the use of *between* and *among:* "One of [the computer artist's] big assignments in *The Phantom Menace* was working on the light-saber battle among Jedi knights Qui-Gon Jinn and Obi-Wan Kenobi and the evil Darth Maul" (*Lexington Herald-Leader*). We often encounter an old superstition here—that you can't say *between* if more than two persons or parties are involved in a situation. Certainly *among* would be fine in the quoted sentence if each of the three were battling the other two, but if it's the two knights on one side versus the evil Darth on the other, then it's a battle *between* two contending forces.

Besides, *between* has never in its history been restricted to just two entities. As the *Oxford English Dictionary* explains, *between* is "the only word available to express the relation of a thing to many surrounding things severally and individually." We speak of a treaty *between* five countries, for instance, because each country has an individual obligation to every other country. *Among,* however, has the basic meaning of *in the midst of* or *surrounded by* and always refers in one way or another to a group.

Those Good Old Sayings {39}

Seeming only vaguely familiar with old sayings and figures of speech, media figures often emasculate these traditional gems before uttering them. High-powered lawyers on CNN crime and scandal shows, my grouchy friend notes, not only have frequent trouble with subject-verb agreement but are given to such observations as "what's *good* for the goose is good for the gander." *Good* for! What happened to *sauce:* "What's *sauce* for the goose"? If no sauce is available, who needs a goose anyway? (The grouch reminds us that one of the chief reasons for preserving old sayings is simply that they add spice—indeed, *sauce*—to language.)

This piece of revisionism appears minor, however, when we compare it with an extraordinary observation (quoted in the *Boston Globe*) by a Harvard professor of public health who referred to the federal Family and Medical Leave Act as grossly inadequate but, nevertheless, "an important toe in the doorstep." From *foot* in the *door* (picture an aggressive door-to-door salesman) to *toe* in the *doorstep?* In reality, of course, even if you could somehow manage to drive your toe into a doorstep the only result would be an extremely sore toe. You wouldn't come close to getting inside the house.

A less dramatic but equally strange alteration of another old expression came from a campaign colleague of Senator John McCain's. Praising the senator's efforts to move the Republicans toward the political center, the colleague declared: "He has his *pulse* on where the majority of the people are more than the party does." It's impossible to imagine what mental picture this politician could have been contemplating when he uttered this sentence, but he clearly was not thinking about fingers resting on a pulsating blood vessel, as he would have been had he said that the senator had "his *fingers on the pulse* . . ."

Reviewing American policies in relation to violence in the world, a professor commented: "We've created and engendered such hostilities with our policies over five decades. You can't just turn the *spicket* off *with* violence." The professor was talking informally in an interview, and he no doubt meant to speak of turning off the *spigot of* violence. But *spicket?* That—also no doubt—was the contribution of the reporter taking notes. It has a fine Middle English or Old English ring to it, but such a ring is quite false; the truth is surely that the reporter, unfamiliar with the word *spigot*, didn't bother to look it up. Or, of course, he may have tried but got nowhere with his spelling of the word.

A failure of imagination also marked this comment by a con-scientious social worker, disturbed by the inadequacy of services for the poor, who fretted about the fate of people who "fall *between* the cracks." If you fall between the cracks, of course, you won't go very far at all because you'll hit something solid; try falling "*through* the cracks."

Old expressions also suffer from quite minor alterations. An eminent basketball coach, for instance, responded with restraint but with an omitted *-ed* to the sight of four of his undergraduate players being scooped up in the National Basketball Association draft. Said the coach: "It's not cut and *dry*, but overall I would side with finishing [school] and graduating and growing and all of that."

As the grouch noted, what we miss here is the idea of process—of metaphorical timber being first cut and then *dried* and thus being rendered ready for use. There's nothing puzzling about the meaning, but the figure of speech suffers.

In the same way, the action fades when an antiques columnist speaks of "16-ounce *ice* tea glasses, for $9.99 each postpaid," and a writer on interior decorating describes how seamlessly, in one TV apartment, "furniture from the 1930s blends with '90s pieces laid out over a gorgeous 1920s floral *hook* rug." Since such a rug is made by hooking, it is a *hooked* rug, and the tea is properly called *iced*, because it is cooled by the application of ice.

I close this topic with a reference to the late union president Jimmy Hoffa. Attempting to quiet speculation in the press that an associate of Hoffa's was involved in the disappearance of the Teamster president, the associate's lawyer said firmly that if his client "knew anything about it, he'd be *deader than a doughnut 25 years ago.*" In view of what's supposed to have happened to Hoffa, that thought makes a plain old *doornail* seem something to be envied.

THE GROUCH'S REMINDER

Old sayings play an important part in keeping language colorful and interesting, and they remind us that we have a past. Take the trouble to get them right.

Fuzz {40}

Uncertain, fuzzy use of language, as if the writer were playing a game with which he or she was not wholly familiar, often gives the grouchy grammarian a great deal of concern. He had a little scrawled note to that effect on this muddled and hence hard-to-understand paragraph from an AP story: "Never the types who are satisfied until every angle has been covered, Vince McMahon and Dick Ebersol get right back to work this week with one task in mind: Make sure the XFL was not a one-shot wonder."

Did the writer really mean to suggest that McMahon and Ebersol are not concerned about covering every angle? Surely not. Surely he meant that the two gentlemen—never mind the "types"—are not satisfied *until* or *unless* they have covered every angle. If he wanted to preserve the structure he had, he could have said *before* instead of *until*. (Despite McMahon's and Ebersol's devotion, however, their new football league soon folded.)

Many people sitting at keyboards will go to considerable lengths to avoid being firm and unequivocal; they seem to strive for an astigmatic, out-of-focus effect. Discussing the dispute in an Alabama town over a statue of a Confederate general, an AP reporter declared, "Both sides of the issue seemed *confident* there *might be* a compromise." No, no, that's not it! They *thought* there *might* be a compromise, or they were *confident* there *would be* one. And notice how often you hear such sentences as "I'm *sure* she's *probably* the one you mean" and "I *definitely* think he *may* get the job." If you're sure and definite, you're not thinking *probably* and *maybe*, but, unfortunately, we seem to have become a nation of speakers and writers who hedge our bets.

Here's a spectacular case of equivocation. On a memo page of sentences he jotted down from a Los Angeles television report concerning a body found at the foot of a cliff, the grouch had scribbled "incredible" opposite this statement: "Authorities are unsure if the woman *may have fell*." (*May* is, of course, only part of the focus problem here.)

THE GROUCH'S REMINDER

Fuzzy speech is unpersuasive, unconvincing speech. Make your meaning clear.

As . . . Than {41}

As we have seen over and over, professional users of English frequently display carelessness toward some of the simple operating principles of the language, if not actual ignorance of them. This failing, indeed, has constituted one of the themes of this book.

A typical example comes from a *Hartford Courant* story on causes of death for teachers: "Autoimmune diseases are more than twice as likely to strike women *than* men." A National Public Radio reporter who was discussing changes in the housing market offered another typical example. During the latest quarter, she said, financial institutions had made "twice as many home loans *than* in" the comparable quarter a year earlier.

Once again, we point out that we have *more than* or *less than* somebody else has, all right, but this time we add that bankers made twice *as many* loans *as* they made earlier. It's surprising that the reporter's ear didn't tell her that "twice as many *than*" didn't work. Or that the Hartford reporter didn't see his problem either: The diseases were more than twice as likely to strike women *as* [to strike] men.

According to another NPR reporter, "black students are three times as likely to be targeted for special education *than* whites." And still a third NPR reporter used the phrase "as much . . . *than*" for "as much . . . *as*." Quite surprising, indeed. (Neither the grouch nor his colleague has anything against National Public Radio; in fact, quite the contrary is true. The same goes, of course, for all the other leading institutions cited in this book.)

Perhaps these two lines can serve as a kind of shorthand guide:

as likely (or *popular, thoughtful, idiotic,* etc.) *as*

more likely (or *popular, thoughtful, idiotic,* etc.) *than*

In this same little corner of language, we frequently look in vain for a needed *as*: "'All signs indicate "Survivor" is just as popular, if not more popular, than when the second edition ended,' CBS spokesman Chris Ender said" (AP). "Just as popular *as*" is what we need here, with the second comma moved one word to the right.

This corner also has room for one more example, this time of the absence of a much-needed *than*. Discussing in his *New York Times Magazine* column the growing importance of the phrase *optical semiconductor* (and of the thing it stands for), William Safire noted that "a regular semiconductor, like the chip in today's computers, is based on electricity, but an optical semiconductor is based on light, *of* which nothing is faster." Nothing is faster *of* light? What appears to be needed here is that friendly old workhorse, *than*.

Not Appropriate {42}

O ne morning, pawing through a file drawer marked MALAPROPISMS, I turned up an article that had me chuckling for the rest of the day. *Malapropism* comes from Mrs. Malaprop, a pretentious and gabby character in the eighteenth-century play *The Rivals*, by Richard Brinsley Sheridan; her name, in turn, comes from the French *mal à propos*—inappropriate.

More than a mere mispronunciation, a malapropism is a wildly inappropriate rendering of a word or expression, a veritable mangling, and it is customarily created by someone who is speaking for effect. Mrs. Malaprop, the original, won her eternal fame with such lines as this: "If I reprehend any thing in this world, it is the use of my oracular tongue, and a nice derangement of epitaphs." She described another character as being "as headstrong as an allegory on the banks of the Nile," and she thought that "illiterate" was a verb meaning "eliminate." (No doubt, all of these seemed fresher and funnier a couple of centuries ago.)

Mrs. Malaprop has had countless worthy real-life successors through the years since she made her appearance, one of the finest being the World War II patriot who staunchly cried: "Remember Pearl Island!" And the wife of the late Kingsley Amis once assured a friend that if he should enjoy success in a certain endeavor, "the world's your lobster." But no examples can exceed those I found in the grouch's file drawer. Not only are they funny, they offer the strongest possible proof that one should actually think about what one is saying. Look at these examples, all of them from government officials:

He said it off the top of his cuff.

Now we've got to flush out the skeleton.

He deals out of both ends of his mouth.

Don't rock the trough.

A study is under foot.

The project is going to pot in a handbasket.

He has worked at several places. He just put in a stench at HEW.

They treated him as if he had the Blue Bonnet plague.

And note this insightful observation on a pioneering effort of some kind: *We're breaking pre-virgin territory.*

Can't deal with a problem? That's all right—you can do as one bureaucrat suggested to another: *Since we can't handle it now, let's leave it to prosperity.*

There's also this comment in a friendly note written by a bureaucrat to a colleague making an all-out effort against a rival: *Going for the juggler again, eh, Art?*

I found that line particularly poignant, as I imagined an innocent entertainer tossing his clubs in the air and then being crushed onstage by a savage onslaught from one of the wings. What could this civil servant possibly have done to bring such a violent fate on himself?

If you strongly object to a proposal, you can tell your colleagues: *We can shoot potholes in that argument.* You might even say: *I'm not going to bail out his chestnuts.*

And, if things don't go your way, you can simply drive off in your extremely snazzy *Fiat accompli.*

One disgusted worker derided the boss with this crack: *He likes sitting there in his big executive snivel chair.*

Sometimes a person seems to speak out of a dense fog, like the Michigan legislator who declared, with surely unintended candor: "I don't think people appreciate how difficult it is to be a pawn of labor." A colleague warned members of the opposing party: "From now on I'm watching everything you do with a fine-toothed comb." Another issued a frank and memorable appeal to his fellows: "Let's violate the law one more year."

A legislator from an unnamed state entered the fray with a truly thunderous declaration: "If we don't stop shearing the wool of the sheep that lays the golden egg, we'll pump it dry"—a condition in which he may well have found himself after that remarkable utterance.

Although not a member of any legislature, Lucy Lawless, the New Zealand–born star of the TV adventure program *Xena*, proved the equal of any American senator or representative with this description of her feelings when the series concluded: "After *Xena* ended in April, I had to take a break. I felt like I had been chasing a greased pig, trying to grab the brass ring in pursuit of the holy grail in Hollywood."

Discussing a football coach's quest for the 300th victory in his long career, a sportswriter on a small-town (and therefore unmentioned) newspaper commented: "Although [the coach] would have preferred putting the milestone on the back burner, he is tickled with the chance to reach the 300-win club on his own turf." Earlier he had spoken of No. 300 as "the elusive milestone." It's not hard to see that this writer had no pictures of a milestone or a burner or anything else in his head and was merely putting down words.

Despite its population of scientific and engineering types, Silicon Valley has produced a good bit of similar out-of-focus speech, much of which has tended to show up in company

meetings. "If we keep going on this way," one computer professional warned his associates, "somebody is going to be left standing at the church with his pants down." Another explained a
female colleague's view by saying that "she had a missed conception." Other scrambled clichés: "That's just putting the gravy
on the cake," "That's the whole kettle of fish in a nutshell," "He
flew it by ear." (And, the grouch noted in a little addendum,
"everybody should remember that it's *Silicon* Valley, not *Silicone*."
I had to smile at that, since I've encountered that mistake, too.)

You will note that most of the preceding instances consist of
figures of speech. But beyond obvious metaphors and similes, we
often encounter other words or expressions that may once have
been metaphorical and, though having lost that status, are still a
bit beyond the literal.

A writer in the *Baltimore Sun* noted, for instance, that "the
stigma against mental illness prevails." But, originally, a stigma
was a scar or a mark (the most famous stigmata being, of course,
those of Christ) and figuratively it still is. Hence *stigma* is not a
synonym for disapproval or prejudice but is instead a property of
the person or trait that is the object of such disapproval. The *Sun*
writer should probably have avoided the metaphor altogether
and simply said *prejudice*.

I found especially interesting a clipping, filed without comment by the grouch, from a 1914 *New York Times*. Wondering
how my friend had acquired such an old item and why he had
preserved it, I noted the heading F. BLUMENTHAL DIES AT
SEA, and then the rather surprising subhead: "Old Leather Merchant Was a Collector of Antiques and Paintings." All right, I
thought after a moment's reflection, this merchant must have
specialized in goods made of old leather (whatever they may
have been), and the newspaper had simply omitted the needed
hyphen. But since the text then described him as "one of the old-
est merchants in the leather business," I decided that the age of
the company must be what was meant. The article made no

explicit mention of the age of the deceased himself, however, and I then wondered whether "old" might not actually refer to Blumenthal himself. Either way, the wording in the piece offered a striking example of the kinds of almost unnoticeable changes that continually occur in language and taste (changes the grouchy grammarian does not, by the way, deny). Even in an era less touchy and given to euphemism than ours, ambiguously employed words like "old" would hardly appear in an obituary notice.

Sometimes it may all become a bit too much for the hard-working speaker or writer, who may find himself or herself sharing the outlook of the mother of several highly active children. One day this young woman declared in some desperation, "My kids are going to drive me to an early drink."

THE GROUCH'S REMINDER

Figures of speech represent mental pictures. When you use such a figure, try to see the image that goes with it.

Sorry, You've Already Used That One {43}

As one of the best customers of his nearby health-food store, my grouchy friend is a regular consumer of fruits grown without pesticides and meats free of infused hormones and antibiotics. His devotion to these "organic" products comes naturally, I think; he was talking with fervor about the organic nature of the sentence long before the natural-foods movement came along to put the word *organic* into common use. For him, it offers a convenient way of expressing his belief that every sentence has its requirements—the right words—which must be met. And the sentence must have *all* the words it needs as well.

Hence he made a notation to this effect on a clipping in which a TV critic, describing a program on faith healers, ended with this summation: "When he gets around to his analysis, [the host of the program] suggests that faith that gives comfort is unimpeachable, but also that those who trust faith healers might be more selective *in* whom they place their faith."

What's wrong here? Well, this little word *in* has already finished its work when it has linked the phrase beginning with *whom* to the rest of the sentence, but faith needs an *in*, too—the trusting souls have to place their faith *in* somebody. One *in* simply can't do both jobs. (If you will read the *in* as *concerning* or *when it comes to* or something equivalent, the point becomes obvious.)

In a similar example, an economist is quoted in a *New Yorker* article on American productivity as saying, "No one really knows how much work time is being put in the service sector." *Put in* here serves as the verb, meaning "to spend (time) as indicated," which leaves "service sector" yearning for a preposition to hook it to the rest of the sentence. The economist should have said that nobody knows "how much work is being put in *in* the service sector." That little added *in* serves as the connector. Not an elegant result, perhaps, but perfectly clear.

Although in some contexts even an unexpressed *that* can mean *in which (The Year the Yankees Lost the Pennant)*, the following sentence from a sportswriter's analysis of a college sports investigation would benefit from an explicit *in which:* "[The spokesman] said that the NCAA usually handles cases in the order that they are received, but said that severe cases often take precedence."

The case of a missing *in* (or any other little word) may not be severe, but it definitely deserves attention. I had to chuckle when, more or less idly thinking about this point, I phoned a university library for information about an entirely unrelated subject and was told: "Please wait. Calls are answered in the order they are received." Unfortunately, I was laughing in the ear of a thoroughly unresponsive recording.

THE GROUCH'S REMINDER

Words have their limits. They may do different jobs in a sentence, but they don't like to be asked to do the same job twice.

From Classical Tongues {44}

In telling friends about a concert she had recently attended, a very proper lady couldn't resist complaining about all the noise she had been forced to endure. She and her husband, she said, had seats down front, "right next to the *concussion* section." You might think, at first glance, that mixing up *percussion* and *concussion* is the kind of error that belongs in Topic 37 (Pairs—Some Trickier Than Others), since these two words have the same root. An important difference, however, is that, unlike *historic* and *historical*, they don't represent an established bickering couple. The mistake is an individual scrambling, representing inattention, mind-wandering, or, perhaps, a blind spot that needs a bit of light.

The same principle applies to the complaint of a Chicago lawyer who wrote the *Tribune* to express his objection to a story "in a recent *addition*" of the newspaper. Obviously, the fuddled counselor didn't pause to ask himself: What does the word mean? (This question would represent, in effect, a corollary to the grouch's basic imperative: Think!) Nor was such a question asked by an employer who explained the shrinking of his firm's payroll by saying that "we've been losing employees through *nutrition*."

Percussion, edition, attrition—these and many other familiar words created from Latin roots, prefixes, and suffixes make up much of the stock of our vocabulary, but they can't be useful to us if we don't pay attention to what they really mean. Sound itself does not make a reliable guide.

Even the sounds were not truly close in this implied and unorthodox pair that appeared in a suburban Los Angeles newspaper: "The weekend festival gave people a chance to *divulge* in Greek food, dance and culture." The behind-the-scenes member of the pair, of course, is *indulge*.

Aside from being involved in woolly pairings, words taken from classical languages often seem to pose singular-plural problems. Note these comments by the editor of a retail reporting service, who said of clothing designed for cozy evenings at home: "The *criteria* is that it's comfortable and, most important, washable."

The grouchy grammarian points to a problem here. If *criteria* should become accepted as a singular form, as is often the case and as the editor's use of *is* here suggests, what then would happen to the true singular, *criterion?* Since one of my friend's chief motivations is his fear that needless and ill-informed changes in the language will hurry recent and current literature into obsolescence, if not make it fully obsolete, he notes with urgency the importance of preserving *criterion*. That, after all, was the name of the bar in London into which a recently discharged army surgeon, Dr. John H. Watson, wandered one day in 1881, thereby entering on the series of events that led to his association with Sherlock Holmes and thus to immortality. (The grouch also points out that *criterion* has a valuable specific meaning: it denotes not merely a rule but a standard for judging merit; we may presume, therefore, that the Criterion was an excellent bar.)

A different problem occurs with *kudos*, which comes from the Greek and means the fame, acclaim, or prestige associated with achievement. Because it ends in *s*, people from time to time have thought of it as a plural form and hence, in time, there emerged a "singular" form *kudo* (as in this headline from the *Washington Post:* "Two more *kudos* for Tiger Woods"). This usage is defended, though weakly, by Webster, which declares that it may have begun as a misunderstanding, "but then so did *cherry* and *pea*." The grouchy grammarian would hardly deny that, but he would point out that what happened hundreds of years ago is irrelevant to his present-day concerns. He prefers the crisp conclusion of the *Oxford English Dictionary* concerning *kudos:* "This word is always singular."

My friend also observed in a sidebar that a well-known animal trainer had referred in a TV interview to a cat *specie*, as if this were the singular form and *species* were only the plural. "Hope this kind of thing doesn't become a trend," he noted in the spiky scrawl with which I had become thoroughly familiar.

What does in fact represent a pronounced trend appears in a sentence in *Parade*, which describes how a woman receiving an award "stepped confidently to a *podium* in front of an audience of 500." The honoree may have stepped *onto* a podium (the word, like *podiatrist*, comes ultimately from the Greek word for *foot*), but more likely she stepped *to* a *lectern* (a reading stand—from the Latin for *read*). That's what an MSNBC reporter really meant in saying that "a *podium* was set up" in preparation for a statement by President George W. Bush.

Speaking in a movie review about a character named Romulus (played by Samuel L. Jackson), the writer comments that the character "sleeps under a rocky *enclave* in a Manhattan park." This is pretty grim, because if you're *under* an enclave you're underground—buried—since an enclave is a territory or area completely surrounded by a foreign territory. Since *cave* wouldn't fit here, it isn't quite clear what the writer had in mind.

A book about an event in the early history of North Carolina identified the author as "a *lifetime native* of Carteret County."

Confusion about the meaning of *native* is not at all uncommon. Since the word comes from a Latin verb meaning "to be born," however, it's quite clear that you remain a native whether you stay at home or go far away, and also that the word cannot serve as a synonym for *resident*. (Note the mention of *native* in Topic 6.)

Sound ruled (more or less) over sense in this question from one project official to another: "How should we *amateurize* the cost of the equipment?" These chaps may have been fumbling their way along in an amateurish fashion, all right, but the word needed here was *amortize*, which traces its ancestry back through French to a Latin word meaning "bring to death." You don't merely take care of the mortgage or other kind of debt, you kill it!

A rising trend is yielding such regrettable results as this, from a theater producer: "On June 17, we will celebrate our *tenth-year anniversary*." *Tenth* anniversary by itself will do nicely here; since *anniversary* means "turning of the year" (and, hence, returning annually), no further information is required, and you certainly don't want to display your ignorance unnecessarily. Sometimes this usage appears with a cardinal number instead of an ordinal—*ten*-year anniversary—but it's no more desirable that way. If this trend continues, it will result in *anniversary*'s losing its special significance and becoming merely a synonym for *commemoration* or even *jamboree*.

Imagine the shock Bruce Springsteen and Julianne Phillips felt, some years ago, when they read in a wire-service account of their wedding that this union was sealed "in a *clandestine* ceremony early yesterday." *Clandestine?* The reporter was perhaps expressing his pique that the happy couple managed to keep the wedding secret from the press, but they were getting married, for heaven's sake! The word comes directly from the Latin *clandestinus*, which indeed means secret, but it carries the connotation of illicit, surreptitious, something kept from the knowledge of those entitled to know. The press hardly qualified on that score.

(Probably the most famous employment of the word *clandestine* in the last hundred years came in President John F. Kennedy's October 1962 speech telling the world about the Soviet construction of missile sites in Cuba; it attracted attention not only for itself but because the president pronounced it *clandesTINE*, with the accent on the last instead of the middle syllable.)

Negative impact? That expression represents one of the great paradoxes of the age. Maybe we should speak of an *expact*. If you don't see why, says my crotchety friend, you can either take a cram course in Latin or consult your dictionary. (You'll find that an *impact* is a forceful collision; *expact* is thus just one of my friend's little jokes.)

In a related vein, an NPR business reporter declared that, for the first quarter of 2001, it was "notable that growth was not *negative*." (You can have figures concerning growth that are positive or negative, but you can hardly have negative growth—although you hear about it every day.)

Cogitate is a nice old word we don't hear much any more, but this California scientist appears to have harbored a memory of it somewhere in his mind, even though it emerged in a strikingly different form. "That needs some thinking about," he said to an associate concerning a particular problem. "Let me go away and *regurgitate* for a couple of hours." I think we all know what that means.

Talking about the life and death of Anthony Quinn, the local ABC-TV station in Los Angeles paid the actor a tribute with a uniquely Hollywood flavor. With appropriate awe, the news reader said that Quinn "wrote his *own autobiography*." The word literally means "a life story written by oneself," and thus the reference was a blatant bit of tautology, but who's to say that this young woman dwelling amid the culture of Hollywood didn't know that? Irony? Perhaps, indeed.

THE GROUCH'S REMINDER

Its great vocabulary, drawn from classical, Germanic, and other sources, gives the English language an unrivaled range of expressive power. Take advantage of it by seeing how words are put together.

Like, *Like*   {45}

The way to tell if you are leading is to check behind you for followers. It doesn't sound *like* [your fiancée] has any." So the resident ethicist of the *New York Times Magazine* informed a reader who had some questions about his fiancée's values.

Is the ethicist simply playing fast and loose with the language here, not taking pains to be literate? Instead of making *like* a conjunction, shouldn't he have said *as if* or *as though?* Perhaps, but in this realm the grouch produced a great surprise for me. "Parrish," he said, "you know and I know that everybody in the world, from university dean to university dropout, says 'I felt *like* I was going to die' or 'It sounds *like* he's in big trouble' or 'Wood does not contract *like* steel does.' Everybody! Just look at this clipping." He handed me a story about the tennis player Martina Hingis, who was talking about her need to develop a power game—"in short," said the writer, "to conjure up more easy points *like* the power hitters do."

"Here's another one." My friend passed me a column of household advice by Heloise, who was discussing a photo of two kittens: "They really look *like* they are in step and doing some fancy dancing."

"And," my friend added, "old Porter Perrin, who wrote his

Writer's Guide years ago now, said about *like* and *as:* "Historically both forms are good, since both are parts of the older *like as,*" which appears in the King James Bible.

"Of course I usually don't give a damn about what was true four or five hundred years ago, as you should know, but when genuinely thoughtful people regularly employ a usage today, and such people have employed it through the years, then I have to listen to them. And, damn it, much of the time these people say *like.*

"And what else could you say but 'If You Knew Susie *Like* I Knew Susie'?

"Do I sanction and recommend *like* as a conjunction? Well, Parrish, right now I'm just watching, just listening. But I'm not condemning. . . . Fooled you there, didn't I?" He almost cackled.

Yes, he certainly had fooled me. But had he convinced me? I'm not so sure.

"Back in the nineteen-fifties, in my younger editorial days," said the grouch, "one of the advertising agencies created a furor among the literati when it produced the slogan 'Winston tastes good, *like* a cigarette should.' Everybody was shocked and angry, and Ogden Nash had a poem in the *New Yorker* that declared: '*Like* goes Madison Avenue, *like so* goes the nation.' Many and many a toast was drunk to him for that line.

"But the advertising agency came back with TV commercials that asked the viewers: 'What do you want, good grammar or good taste?' They had what youngsters today call a nerd representing good grammar, with sexy singers and dancers portraying good taste. I fear it wasn't much of a contest!

"Of course it's true, as my friend Margaret Bryant said fifty or sixty years ago in her book *Modern English*, that if you use *like* as a conjunction large segments of the public will regard you as careless or ignorant of the niceties of language. She may have overstated the case a bit, and it's certainly not as true now as it was back in those days. But I tell you that for what it's worth."

My friend concluded our little talk by reminiscing about a poignant twist on *like-as* that was offered in the raucous, slogan-loving 1960s by Vice President Hubert Humphrey, the 1968 Democratic presidential candidate. "Believing that the confusing times and the corrupt world could be explained and redeemed by a few simple slogans," said my friend, "students and others were given to chanting such sayings as 'power to the people' and, to speakers, 'tell it like it is.' Trying to appeal to this large and vocal group, Humphrey, adopting some of the language, went on the air and called on his Republican foes to 'tell it *like* it is.' But that wasn't quite what Humphrey said. Unable to bring himself to use *like* as a conjunction, the vice president cried: "Tell it *as* it is!" Poor Hubert! He just didn't realize that the decade had declared war on usage along with everything else."

As frequently happens in the realm of style and usage, a reverse tendency appears with *like-as*, with *as* being employed where *like* is needed. Here's a clear example from a small-town newspaper: "*As* many people [in such a circumstance], after her brother died Rodgers was left feeling sad and lonely." The writer probably turned to *as* here on the ground of its being higher class than *like* (this idea of an informal class system for words is truly pervasive: *I* and *me*, *he* and *him*, for example). The sentence literally and unintentionally states that Rodgers was serving *in the capacity of* ("as") many people, on the model of "Senator Barkley served as temporary chairman of the convention."

My friend insisted that I make one thing "pellucidly clear," as he likes to say: None of his points concerning *like* should be taken to represent any kind of endorsement of what he calls the teenage or "flibbertigibbet" *like*. By this description he meant the frequent insertion of *like* into sentences as a filler word with no more meaning than a belch ("It's, *like*, getting late"); the use of *like* to mean *about* or *approximately* or even *precisely:* "It's *like* four o'clock"); and the use of *like* to mean *said* ("When he turns to me, I'm *like:* 'Don't ask me'").

THE GROUCH'S REMINDER

For formal purposes, don't use *like* as a conjunction unless you're sure that's what you want to do. It's still not quite respectable in that role.

Just the Facts, Ma'am

Anumber of years ago the laconic statement "Just the facts, ma'am" (a standard line from the famous and long-running TV cop show *Dragnet*) enjoyed quite an extended period of popularity, being said in all kinds of situations, and it seems to have remained a favorite with the grouchy grammarian. Among his folders I found a small one bearing this label, and when I mentioned it to him he urged me to include it as one of the topics. "Even though it wouldn't be about grammar and usage," he said, "we damn well ought to go on record in favor of accuracy. I'm speaking, of course, about accuracy from persons who present themselves as authorities or insiders, and therefore are presumed to know what they're talking about." I readily agreed.

So, for the record, I cite one of the grouch's notes, from a TV program on the *Titanic*. In talking about Mr. and Mrs. Isidor Straus, who were prominent among those passengers who became figures of legend for the manner in which they faced death, the commentator erred by referring to Straus as "the founder of Macy's." Straus was indeed the owner of the store in 1912, but, oddly enough, the business had been founded by a chap named Macy—Rowland H. Macy—in the middle of the nineteenth century; Straus became the owner in 1896. This casual approach to facts might not seem to have much importance in cases like this one, but my friend says simply, "If you're giving facts, give real ones—*actual fact*, as people say. Don't make them up just to save yourself a little time or effort."

An AP story about a book on historical mysteries took up the long-running argument about the authorship of the Shakespearean plays. The writer described the two camps, one supporting Shakespeare himself, the other "populated by proponents of Queen Elizabeth, Roger Bacon, King James, Walter Raleigh, Christopher Marlowe, and even an Arab sheik known as El Spar."

The grouch merely shrugged at the mention of El Spar, but Roger Bacon actually upset him. *Roger* Bacon? Roger Bacon, as everybody used to learn in the fifth or sixth grade, was a thirteenth-century monk and pioneering scientist who is believed to have invented gunpowder. The Bacon who figures in the Shakespeare discussions is Francis Bacon, a contemporary of Shakespeare who achieved eminence both as a philosopher and as a politician. The grouch, who puts little stock in any of the alternative-to-Shakespeare theories, remarked to me that anybody who had read much Bacon could hardly believe him capable of writing anything approaching *King Lear*, *Antony and Cleopatra*, or any of Shakespeare's other works—but, even so, he's entitled to be referred to by his own first name.

Misconceptions disguised as ordinary, everyday facts constitute a special subcategory in this problem area and often turn up in medical and health contexts. Note this photo caption from the *New York Times:* "Valentina, a *former* drug addict and alcoholic, is trying to support herself and three children on a dishwashing job that pays $3.50 an hour." Fortunately, this mother is clean and sober and thus able to make a real attempt to deal with life (enormous as her task is), but it's misleading to speak of her as a *former* alcoholic. Despite various claims by researchers through the years that small, selected groups of alcoholics have successfully practiced social drinking, these groups on closer examination seem to have dissolved, with the supposedly sober drinkers nowhere to be found—no doubt because alcoholism is a medical condition that manifests itself when a person drinks alcohol and does not when a person abstains from it. Therefore Valentina and others in her situation are best described as sober or nondrinking alcoholics.

An obituary notice from northeastern Mississippi crossed the state line to give particulars about a judge from *Mussel* Shoals, Alabama. This soundalike is not uncommon, my friend noted, partly because you would expect to see many more mussels than *muscles* on shoals; nevertheless, the name is *Muscle* Shoals. The grouch also stressed the importance of pointing out this kind of error, because such mistakes are easily made; often they simply represent the easy way out (though looking up a name, he would say, is not necessarily a difficult task).

On the other hand, my friend said, with respect to the facts, one mention usually will do. He noted this on a clipping (from *American Profile*) that made mention of "Antonio Stradivari, an Italian violin-maker born in Italy in 1644." *Born in Italy* is super-fluous there, and it's worth noting because this repetition probably had a mechanical rather than a cerebral cause: the writer put down one thing and then changed her mind but failed to delete the first wording. (But where were the editors and proof-readers? When I put this to my friend, he merely said, "That's not a discussion we need to have now.")

Many such errors and infelicities are the results of the ease with which your computer allows you to make changes, to switch words back and forth for the sake of variety, as you go over your work. (This seems to be particularly true in the singular-plural realm. If you check the verb each time you alter the noun, how-ever, you'll have the satisfaction of knowing that you've made the old grouch not happy, maybe, but a bit more cheerful than he can usually manage.)

• • •

The realm of personal titles presents its own little barriers and traps. A wire-service obituary of an English-born art collector highlighted a common problem for writers and others who do not live in Britain and even for some who do. In describing the career of Sir Arthur Gilbert, the writer gave us this information: "After running a successful evening gown business in England, *Sir Gilbert* retired to Los Angeles at age 36."

Now no one would argue that the English class system with its trappings is a simple affair, but some of the governing principles are actually quite obvious. In speaking of knights, you merely need to think back to Sir Lancelot and his fellows of the Round Table. They were figures of legend, but in actual history a medieval knight was dubbed with his Christian name, and the custom continued no matter how many family and other names followed. Gilbert was therefore *Sir Arthur*, just as the composer Sir Arthur Sullivan was *Sir Arthur* and Sir Winston Churchill was *Sir Winston*. In his 1922 novel *Babbitt*, Sinclair Lewis satirized the people of his fictional midwestern city, Zenith, by having them address a visiting Englishman, Sir Gerald Doak, as *Lord* Doak. Confusingly enough, however, these civic boosters were indeed supposed to address the visitor's wife as *Lady* Doak.

Military titles offer their own complexities. In an informative discussion of the global positioning system, a *New Yorker* writer describes his interview with the commander of the 2nd Space Operations Squadron, Lieutenant Colonel Daniel Jordan. After introducing us to this officer, the writer supplies background information on the G.P.S. and then, returning to his interviewee, says: "*Lieutenant Colonel Jordan*, who was dressed in a crisp blue flight suit, led me around the Master Control Station operations floor"; this style of reference appears several more times. In fact, however, it does not represent the traditional and, indeed, most convenient style; military historians normally do not speak of Lieutenant General Grant, Major General Patton, Brigadier General de Gaulle, or Vice Admiral

Sims. The long-established rule calls for use of the full rank (usually abbreviated) and full name when the individual officer makes his first appearance: Vice Adm. William S. Sims. Subsequently, the officer becomes Admiral Sims (or General Grant, General Patton, General de Gaulle). This simple system has offered clarity and efficiency for many years.

Demonstrating the relentlessness of the media not so much in originally pursuing a story as in keeping it alive and pumped up in print and on the air, the Associated Press reported that one Darrell Condit, the younger brother of Congressman Gary A. Condit, one of the two central figures in Washington's second-biggest intern scandal—the Chandra Ann Levy affair—had been arrested in Fort Lauderdale on "charges of violating *probation* in a 1986 drunken driving case."

Not content with having spread the news about this incident, which of course had nothing to do with the scandal in Washington, the reporter in Fort Lauderdale went on to muddle the story (and to do nothing for Darrell Condit's good name) by referring to a local official's remark that she did not know what violation of *parole* Condit had been charged with. Now probation and parole have marked differences, the most notable of which is that parole is a conditional release from prison before the expiration of one's sentence, whereas if you have been granted probation after being convicted of an offense, you have escaped prison altogether. Thus probation tends to be given to lesser offenders. The two terms certainly ought not to be interchanged; after all, probation is bad enough.

THE GROUCH'S REMINDER

If you're presenting yourself as a person who knows the facts, you have a special obligation to get them right.

Lost Causes? {47}

We come now to a realm in which the grouchy grammarian speaks less from irritation and anger than from studied melancholy. Though I have numbered this topic in the sequence with all the others, it differs from the preceding forty-six because the items here represent beacons, warnings, signs urging us all to unstinting linguistic vigilance. I have picked them merely to demonstrate the kinds of examples my old friend has in mind when he charges us all to do what we can to keep the living alive. In these particular cases, he sadly confesses his fear that the items themselves are not subject to correction or improvement, though he hasn't yet formally declared their cause lost.

The Smithsonian Institution (my friend still gets a quick case of hives when he hears it called the Smithsonian "Institute"), we were informed one day, is planning to seek commercial support for a new project—a "traveling *exhibit*" consisting of a variety of displays. Since this itinerant show will thus be made up of many items, it could better be called a traveling *exhibition*; logically—and traditionally—an exhibit is one item among many in an exhibition or, for that matter, in a courtroom. The grouch does not really expect to win this one, nor do I, but I think we'll both nevertheless feel a jolt when classical DJs begin talking about Mussorgsky's *Pictures at an Exhibit* instead of *Pictures at an Exhibition*.

163

Another fight that both of us have doubts about winning is preservation of the fading distinction between *healthful* and *healthy*. "Use this example," my friend said one day, handing me a clipping from a newspaper supplement. "It's typical." In the column the writer makes a perfectly sound if hardly radical point: "Consistently encouraging physical activity and *healthy* eating habits during childhood will help build these habits for a lifetime." *Healthful* is supposed to mean *promoting* good health, whereas it is *healthy* that means *possessing* good health. The writer quoted here, who no doubt would use *healthy* to mean possessing as well as promoting health, has simply abandoned *healthful*. That's typical, as my friend said, and thus a useful distinction dies in an era that isn't kind to distinctions. They don't even respect it in his favorite health-food store, the grouch snarled.

The nice distinction that existed between *masterful* (dominant) and *masterly* (characterized by skill, in the style of a master) is dying fast, as my friend noted sadly, but he believes that this one still has a bit of life left in it. Even though *masterful* seems to be sweeping all before it, the grouchy grammarian holds on to a slight hope here.

As I had come to see, and as these little examples suggest, my friend opposes, not change itself, but purposeless, muddling, unproductive change. "Words and structures wear out soon enough," he said. "Let's keep the good ones as long as we can, and let's respect their status. Wouldn't you be pleased to see *The Great Gatsby* stay current forever?"

"Yes," I said, thinking back to high school literature textbooks with all those lines of small type crowding the bottoms of the pages, "with no footnotes needed to explain ordinary terms and phrases."

"That's it exactly, Parrish. Not a single damned footnote in the whole book! That's surely an aim worth all your effort."

Surely, indeed.

The Grouch Reflects

Though snarls and fulminations of all kinds represented a way of life for my friend, he didn't always live on the point of exploding. Sometimes he seemed almost philosophical. One afternoon, in the midst of an off-and-on conversation, he suddenly said to me, "Parrish, do you know what the word *quintuplets* means?"

"The five Dionne sisters," I said. "Ontario—nineteen thirty-four."

"Just so. Well, by nineteen thirty-five everybody in the world knew those children and also knew the word. But old Frank Vizetelly—"

"Frank Vizetelly?"

"The editor of the Funk and Wagnalls dictionaries. He was there for years and years, you know. He pointed out one day that up until that time the word *quintuplets* simply meant five things of a kind, but since the previous year it had taken on a very specific meaning: five children born of the same mother at one and the same time."

I had to admit that I had never thought of *quintuplets* as meaning anything else.

"Of course you didn't," he said. "And neither does anybody else nowadays. Vizetelly was using that as an example of the kinds of changes that keep a dictionary compiler on his toes.

Sometimes they happen very quickly. You know what I'm getting at here, don't you? I am damn well aware, Parrish, as much as anybody else, that language grows and changes. People who say I'm not are simply ignorant and wrong. But I also think about and honor those who love language and have been defending it in rear-guard actions for years. And I think that each of us can play a part in shaping it.

"You know, once, back in my much younger days, the *New York Times* had an editorial they titled 'English at Bay.' They were attacking some poor professor who had written a book about words, because he liked *brass tacks*, *sob-stuff*, *wow*, and *washout*, but what was amusing was that two or three weeks later they had a letter from a very distinguished citizen who was surprised that they had merely spoken of the language's being at bay. For him, matters were in much worse shape than that. He said—the clipping's in there somewhere—'I very much fear English is on the run.'

"Of course we need new words and new uses for old words, Parrish. But which words, and in which contexts, on which levels? And which usages? And what does *need* mean? You know, don't you, that those were some of the real questions in the great eruption that came twenty-five years after that professor and his book."

"The great eruption?" What on earth was my friend talking about?

"The publication, in 1961, of Webster's Third International, that's what I'm talking about! You can use any figure of speech you want: it was an eruption, it exploded like a bomb, it blew the top off the house of lexicography. I've never seen anything like it. They'd been working on this dictionary since they put out the second edition in 1934, but the *Times* satirized it in an editorial—" He interrupted himself, chuckling, then said, "The *Times* editors referred to the editors up in Springfield as 'a passel of double-domes,' using those and other words that Webster had just declared to be proper English. No, not proper English, since there wasn't supposed to be such a thing anymore. Just English. Then the American Heritage company tried to buy Merriam-Webster so they could put out an acceptable new dictionary. The *Library Journal* and the American Bar Association and the *Saturday Review* and the *New Republic* all piled on. Dwight Macdonald eviscerated the Third International in a long analytical article in the *New Yorker,* and in *Harper's,* or maybe it was the *Atlantic,** Wilson Follett called the whole thing 'sabotage in Springfield.' And the war's been going on ever since.

"Phil Gove, the editor of the Third International, said that a dictionary has no business dealing in what he called artificial notions of correctness or superiority—it should be descriptive and not prescriptive. Well, Parrish, that's where you and I came in, isn't it? One fellow said at the time, 'Hell, if they don't tell you what's right, what's the point in having the thing at all?' Even though I'll admit that the dictionary has many virtues, the fellow had a valid complaint, I think. For many persons, a dictionary is a manual of practical correctness, just like the book you're working on now. If you're writing a school paper or a business letter or a legal brief, you want to know what thoughtful users of the language would say about your question, don't you?

"I remember that one writer took the word *bimonthly* as his example. It had always meant every two months but now Webster said that because some people used it to mean twice a month, that was just as good a use. What this meant was that the word became so ambiguous that it lost any meaning; what could have less value than an ambiguous word about time? It's true to this day: If somebody tells you that a publication comes out bimonthly, you have to ask how often that is. So you couldn't settle a bet about a word any more by looking it up in the dictionary.

*It was the *Atlantic.*

"But all this did have a point for Gove and his collaborators. It was supposed to be anti-elitist and democratic and antihistorical."

I wanted to get into the act. "Yes, sir, I know. For them it represented the synchronic approach shoving out the diachronic. The descriptive defeating the historical."

"That's right, Parrish. History no longer mattered. I suppose I'm not exactly surprised at you for understanding that, but . . ." He humphed. "In any case, for those practitioners it was perfectly valid, because they see the study of language as a form of anthropology. Usage? Whose usage? Anybody's. For their abstract purposes, you see, it doesn't matter. They're playing a different game. But of course it does matter to the fellow who wants to write that important letter or settle the bet or ghost-write a presidential address. I certainly hope that whoever that person may be, he or she, adult or child, will find some help in your book."

I hope so, too.

Afterword

My first look at our local newspaper one Sunday morning gave me a glow of righteousness. Our cause was indeed just! I held the evidence right there in my hand.

A number of months—two seasons, half a year—had passed since my early spring conversations with the grouchy grammarian. Just the day before, I had stopped by to see him, proudly bearing the manuscript of this book. Wondering what he would think of my work, and a little concerned about his possible reaction to some of the details in my picture of him, I was awaiting his call. We had moved into late October now, and as I slid the paper from its plastic sleeve I noted the banner across the top of page one: DAYLIGHT SAVINGS TIME ENDED AT 2 A.M. DID YOU SET YOUR CLOCKS BACK ONE HOUR?

I had to laugh. In April we had sprung forward with a superfluous *s*, and now, many notes and clippings later, we had fallen back with that same detested *s*. Now I could forget any worries about my old friend's possible sensitivity to anything I had said. I knew that as soon as he saw the paper he would be on the phone, spurred by that banner head and not by any thoughts about his own image. He would waste no time in chitchat. He would drive straight to the point, telling me that the need for the book was even more urgent than he had come to believe during the summer—"Just look at that damned headline, Parrish!"— and he would order me to see that it made a quick appearance in print. I would say, of course, that I would certainly do my best.

Using This Book

The *Grouchy Grammarian* is intended to be read for information and even for entertainment. Hence it is a narrative as well as a reference book—a manual of practical correctness, as noted earlier, with the aim of helping those who read it improve their communication with other persons. Beyond that, the grouch hopes it will do its small part to preserve existing literature by helping it remain readable for future generations. We also see still another purpose: to help readers gain insight into themselves by increasing the clarity of their thinking.

You may read the topics in any order or no order, though Topic 1 is really the cornerstone of the whole book and you probably will benefit from consulting it early in your reading.

The easiest way to check on a particular point is to turn to the index, which knits the book together and, in particular, serves as a handy and quick finder for any word, phrase, or idea.

Since the book is presented as a how-not-to manual, the examples it offers are almost all negative. We took this approach for good reason: As the Fowler brothers wrote a century ago, "Something may really be done for the negative virtues by mere exhibition of what should be avoided." Besides, this approach offers the most fun, but simple courtesy requires us to state that (as is surely obvious) frequent mention in these pages of any publication, news-gathering enterprise, or broadcasting network does not mean that this concern makes more mistakes than others; quite the opposite is most likely true. The sources appear here because, as leaders in their fields, they are the ones the grouchy grammarian and his colleague most frequently read or listen to.

Thanks

T he grouchy grammarian, and I as his associate, wish to express our gratitude to friends who, with ideas and in other ways, have helped us with this book: Nancy Daniel, Nina James Fowler, George Graves, Ted Levitt, Claudia Miller, Audrey O'Neill, Diane Parrish, Alberta Rifkin, Alec Rooney, Audrey Rooney, Ellen Stevens, Nancy Coleman Wolsk, and Jeremy Wolsk. I am especially grateful to Ilene McGrath for her comments. Each of these persons, as promised, is receiving the widely coveted Grouchy Grammarian T-shirt.

I also wish to express my appreciation for the interest taken in the book by the late Sam Stevens, and I further wish to mention three reporters—Eugene Carlson, Lawrence Harrison, and Daniel Mintz—who, in articles written long ago that are now only yellowed newsprint in the grouch's files, displayed a sharp eye for the incongruous and the unintentionally funny. I have never met these gentlemen, but I wish to express my admiration for these three stories.

I thank Sam P. Burchett, Esq., for legal counsel and David Miller for technical help in the computer realm.

For the commendable perspicacity he displayed in taking a liking to the grouchy grammarian and for his work in bringing my friend to public attention, I express my deep appreciation to my editor, Chip Rossetti. Thanks also to his colleague at John Wiley & Sons, Marcia Samuels, who shepherded the book through production and seemed to enjoy the task.

For all his services, I am as always grateful to my ever efficient, ever cheerful agent, Stuart Krichevsky. I appreciate, also, the help of his assistant, Shana Cohen.

I thank my good friend and fellow author Charles Bracelen Flood for his continuing advice and encouragement.

Finally, I wish to make mention of my dear friend Nancy Coleman Wolsk, who, as noted above, is receiving a Grouchy Grammarian T-shirt and is also receiving love and thanks from me.

From the Grouch's Shelves
A Bibliography

Of the many works on language and related subjects that fill the grouchy grammarian's shelves, a number show signs of particularly heavy consultation through the years, and hence can be considered to have made important contributions to my friend's thinking. Among these are H. W. Fowler's *Modern English Usage* (in its original [1926], second corrected [1937], and revised [by Sir Ernest Gowers—1965] editions) and also the latest incarnation of this famous book, published as *The New Fowler's Modern English Usage*, edited by R. W. Burchfield (1996). My friend has also made much use of the Fowler brothers' (H. W. and F. G.) earlier (1906; third edition, 1931) classic work *The King's English*. (All the Fowler volumes are published by the Oxford University Press.)

The list includes, as well, two other outstanding dictionaries of usage—*A Dictionary of Contemporary American Usage*, by Bergen Evans and Cornelia Evans (well worth an extensive search in secondhand bookstores—Random House, 1957; reprinted by Galahad Books, 1981), and *Modern American Usage*, by Wilson Follett, edited and completed by Jacques Barzun et al. (Hill and Wang, 1966).

• • •

Also important are:

The Complete Plain Words, by Sir Ernest Gowers—an assault on "officialese" by a civil servant who also revised Fowler (David R. Godine, 1988);

Classics in Linguistics, a collection made up of contributions from some of the leading twentieth-century scholars in the field—Otto Jespersen, Leonard Bloomfield, George L. Kittredge, Noam Chomsky, and others (Philosophical Library, 1967);

The Chicago Manual of Style, all editions, from the eleventh (1949) to the present, of this standard handbook for publishers and editors (University of Chicago Press);

Brewer's Dictionary of Phrase and Fable, the centenary edition, revised by Ivor H. Evans (Harper, 1970).

Among other volumes of varying vintages that regularly attracted my roving eye were:

The King's English, by Kingsley Amis—this notable novelist's last book (St. Martin's, 1997);

The Complete Stylist, by Sheridan Baker. "Slips in grammar," the author reminds us, "can only distract your reader from what you are saying, and start him thinking, unflatteringly, about you." (Thomas Y. Crowell, 1966);

Grammar and Good Taste, by Dennis E. Baron—an account, by a nonreformer, of two centuries of American attempts to reform the language (Yale University Press, 1982);

Simple & Direct, by Jacques Barzun—a classic from a classic thinker (Harper, 1975);

The Careful Writer, by Theodore M. Bernstein—a handbook by a language guru who based himself at the *New York Times* (Atheneum, 1965);

Miss Thistlebottom's Hobgoblins by Theodore M. Bernstein (Farrar, Straus and Giroux, 1971);

Words on Words, by John B. Bremner—"In a no-fault society," the author complains, "not much is being done to stay the surge of literary barbarism" (Columbia University Press, 1980);

Words and Things, by Roger Brown (Free Press, 1958);

Modern English and Its Heritage, by Margaret M. Bryant—a good look at thought about grammar and usage in the mid-twentieth century (Macmillan, 1948);

Mother Tongue, by Bill Bryson (Morrow, 1990);

The English Language, by Robert Burchfield—reflections on the "pedigree and credentials" of the language by the editor of the *Oxford English Dictionary* (Oxford University Press, 1985);

Unlocking the English Language, by Robert Burchfield (Hill and Wang, 1991);

The Tyranny of Words, by Stuart Chase—the famous book that long ago introduced many readers to the subject of semantics (Harcourt, Brace, 1938);

Ferocious Alphabets, by Denis Donoghue (Faber and Faber, 1981);

The Highly Selective Dictionary for the Extraordinarily Literate, by Eugene Ehrlich (HarperCollins, 1997);

The HarperCollins Concise Dictionary of English Usage, by Eugene Ehrlich and Daniel Murphy (1991);

Teaching English, by Tricia Evans (Croom Helm, 1982);

A Handbook of Revision, by Norman Foerster and J. M. Steadman, Jr.—The student of writing is told precisely what's what in this compact but thorough and wide-ranging handbook; Foerster was a prominent critic and author during the 1920s and 1930s, and he and his colleague unflinchingly use terms like *impropriety* and *vulgarism* to set wayward writers straight (Houghton Mifflin, 1931);

A Dictionary of Modern American Usage by Bryan A. Garner—a contemporary landmark (Oxford University Press, 1998);

A Dictionary of Modern Legal Usage, by Bryan A. Garner (Oxford University Press, 1987; second edition, 1995);

The Use and Abuse of the English Language, by Robert Graves and Alan Hodges—the wisdom and wit one would expect from Graves (Jonathan Cape, 1943; Marlowe & Company edition, 1995);

Words and Their Ways in English Speech, by J. B. Greenough (Macmillan, 1929);

The Use and Misuse of Language, edited by S. I. Hayakawa, with contributions by Gregory Bateson, Edmund Glenn, and others, as well as by the editor (Harper, 1962);

The State of the Language, by Philip Howard (Oxford University Press, 1985);

A Word in Your Ear, by Philip Howard—quite a few words, actually, from *adultery* to *wizard* (Oxford University Press, 1983);

The Miracle of Language, by Charlton Laird (World, 1953);

The Uses of English, by Herbert J. Muller (Holt, Rinehart and Winston, 1967);

Woe Is I, by Patricia T. O'Conner (Putnam, 1996);

The Opdycke Lexicon of Word Selection, by John B. Opdycke—a work bearing the marvelous subtitle "Illustrative Studies in Dictional Precision for Speakers and Writers" (Funk & Wagnalls, 1950);

Say What You Mean, by John B. Opdycke (Funk & Wagnalls, 1944);

Usage and Abusage, by Eric Partridge—arranged alphabetically and intended to "supplement and complement" Fowler (Hamish Hamilton, 1957 edition; Penguin, 1963);

Dictionary of Linguistics, by Mario Pei and Frank Gaynor (Philosophical Library, 1954);

Pinckert's Practical Grammar, by Robert C. Pinckert (Writer's Digest Books, 1986);

Our Language, by Simeon Potter (Penguin, 1950);

Dictionary of Phrase and Allusion, by Nigel Rees (Bloomsbury, 1991);

The Survival of English, by Ian Robinson—essays concerned with how language either fosters or debases the values of the community (Cambridge University Press, 1973);

The Need for Words, by Patsy Rodenburg (Routledge, 1993);

In Praise of English, by Joseph T. Shipley (Times Books, 1977);

The New York Times Manual of Style and Usage, by Allan M. Siegal and William G. Connolly—the official, very accessible guide for those writing and editing the "newspaper of record," as the *Times* is generally and justly considered (Times Books, 1999);

Introduction to English Grammar, by James H. Sledd—a closely reasoned book by an important scholar; not even war, however, could make bedfellows of Professor Sledd and the grouchy grammarian (Scott, Foresman, 1959);

How to Write, by Gertrude Stein—Gertrude Stein? Yes, it was startling, indeed, to see this idiosyncratic literary stylist in such sober company, but at one point she does say, winningly, "A grammarian there is a pleasure in the air . . ." (original edition, 1931; issued in America by Something Else Press, 1973);

The Elements of Style, by William Strunk, Jr., and E. B. White—the classroom rules of White's old English teacher at Cornell, revived and buttressed by White and thus reborn as a perennial best-seller (Macmillan, 1959; 3rd edition, 1979);

Transformational Grammar and the Teacher of English, by Owen Thomas (Holt, Rinehart and Winston, 1965);

Cross-Talk in Comp Theory, edited by Victor Villaneuva, Jr. (National Council of Teachers of English, 1997);

A Desk Book of Errors in English, by Frank H. Vizetelly—the longtime editor of Funk & Wagnalls dictionaries tells readers how to use "the right word in the right place" (Grosset & Dunlap, 1906; revised edition, 1920);

The Columbia Guide to Standard American English, by Kenneth G. Wilson (Columbia University Press, 1993).

Dictionaries occupy considerable space in the grammarian's study. The list includes the *Oxford English Dictionary* (the familiar *OED*); *Webster's Third New International Dictionary; Merriam-Webster's Collegiate Dictionary* (1936, 1953, 1967, 1973, 1994); the *Oxford American Dictionary;* and the *Random House Dictionary.*

The first time the grouchy grammarian caught me at my browsing, he quickly informed me that of course he didn't wholly agree with the opinions of any of these authors or editors. I assured him that this news hardly surprised me.

Index